★ ★ ★ ★

This book belongs to

_____

*a young woman who
wants to follow Jesus*

A
Young
Woman
Who Reflects
the Heart
of Jesus

Elizabeth George

HARVEST HOUSE PUBLISHERS

EUGENE, OREGON

Cover by Dugan Design Group, Bloomington, Minnesota

Cover photos © Jeanne Hatch, Rouven Maccario / Fotolia

A YOUNG WOMAN WHO REFLECTS THE HEART OF JESUS
Copyright © 2011 by Elizabeth George
Published by Harvest House Publishers
Eugene, Oregon 97402
www.harvesthousepublishers.com

Library of Congress Cataloging-in-Publication Data
George, Elizabeth, 1944-
A young woman who reflects the heart of Jesus / Elizabeth George.
    p. cm.
ISBN 978-0-7369-3042-0 (pbk.)
1. Teenage girls—Religious life. 2. Christian teenagers. I. Title.
BV4551.3.G463 2011
248.8'33—dc22

2010050121

Printed in the United States of America

11 12 13 14 15 16 17 18 19 / VP-NI / 10 9 8 7 6 5 4 3 2 1

Contents

★ ★ ★ ★

An Invitation to...
Become More Like Jesus

Dear Friend,

If you are even holding this book in your hands, I already know you are special! That's because you must be interested in Jesus. Maybe, like me, you want with all your heart to become more and more like Him. Well, good news! This book is packed with information and help that will show you how to move further down the path toward growing more like Jesus. As we walk that path together, here are a few things that will make the journey even sweeter.

*Open your book...*and enjoy it! It's just a book. And I wrote it so you can carry it with you and learn more about your Savior in little bits here and there. So put it in your backpack by day, and on your nightstand when you get home. If you're going on a trip, take it along. You don't need your Bible because I've included plenty of verses right in the book to help you know more about Jesus. And you don't need to answer any questions if you're not able to or don't want to while you are reading. Just read it like you would any other book and let the truths about Jesus do their transforming work as they flood into your heart.

Open your heart... to your friends. Encourage them to get books too. Then you will each be growing, which means your friendships will grow in the right direction—in the things of the Lord. So invite others to join you. I can only imagine the great talks you'll have about Jesus!

Open your heart... and look around. Are there any girls you don't know very well—at school, in your neighborhood, or even in your youth group at church—who you can invite to join you in your study? Girls who need the Savior? Who need guidelines and role models like Jesus for their lives? Who need a friend—like you and Jesus? Whisper a prayer to God and be bold. Reach out and invite someone to get together with you, someone you would like to know better—and someone you would like to help know Jesus better.

Open your heart... to the Savior. Let Him show you the way to live, how to treat people, how to love others, how to be a great daughter and sister, and how to grow into a godly young woman. Let Him tell you what a wonderful creation you are because you know Him!

Open your heart... through prayer to the Holy Spirit. Ask Him to make His Word clear. Ask Him to help you understand your relationship with Jesus and the importance of following Him with all your heart.

Open your heart... and dream! Dream of the woman you yearn to be—a woman who reflects the character of Jesus.

And now let's put feet on those dreams! It is the prayer of my heart that the contents of this book about Jesus, the most special Person who ever lived, will encourage you, excite you, instruct you, and inspire you to love Him even more passionately.

In His great and amazing love,
Your friend and sister in Christ,

Elizabeth George

1

Confident
You Can Do It!

Jessica's confidence (which wasn't very high to begin with!) was slipping even further down the scale toward rock bottom. She hadn't always been so fearful. It all started last month when she had to give a report after her American history class had taken a field trip to the state capital. She had frozen during her speech, forgotten most of what she was supposed to say, and made a complete fool of herself as she stumbled through her report. (Never mind that she had slapped her report together during study hall and hadn't even glanced at it before giving her speech!)

Then there was the incident near her locker, when she tried to defend another girl from some hateful comments made by a mean-girl group that was bullying the poor girl because of the clothes she was wearing. (True, they were a little odd, but they were nothing that deserved the treatment this gang of girls dished out.) *Boy,* Jessica thought afterward, *did they ever let me have it for interfering! Now I'm on their mean list for sure, and that's not a list I wanted to be on!*

And Jessica still regretted her run-in with Tiffany, one of the "cool girls," who asked her face-to-face, "Are you one of those Christian goodie-two-shoes?" Knowing full well it would be the end of her chance for a cool social life, Jessica had said *yes*. (She wasn't so sure about the "goodie" part of the accusation, but she was a Christian and didn't want to lie about it.)

It's no wonder Jessica decided, "Nope, I'm never going to speak up in class again. It's not worth the embarrassment!" With great resolve she added, "And when it comes to speaking up when I see or hear something that's wrong, I'll be minding my own business from now on." Then Jessica concluded with equal firmness, "And for sure when it comes to my Christian faith, I'm gonna keep a low profile. Then maybe no one will ask me about it and ask me questions I can't really answer.

"Nope, I don't want to look like a fool or be embarrassed about anything ever again."

These were the thoughts running through Jessica's mind as she strolled into the youth center for the first meeting of a new Bible study on the life of Jesus.

Reflecting on Confidence

You've probably read or heard about people who have a serious "phobia," an extreme or irrational fear of something. Like these people—and like Jessica—you probably have your very own personal areas of fear or concern about some aspect of life. Now, your "fears" and concerns might not fall in the phobia category, but you are probably like most teens who are very hesitant about certain things because they're just scary for you. Maybe you're uneasy about speaking in public or performing at a recital or in an athletic competition. Or you border on panic when you have an exam. Or you've been studying for your driver's license exam and are wondering how in the world you'll ever remember all those laws and statistics. Whatever your fear is, you are less than confident about participating in that area of concern.

We might not be able to cure you of your area of concern. But as you read on and look at Jesus, you will gain some insight into the importance of trust and learn how it relates to what the Bible says about confidence.

Jesus Shows You the Way

Welcome to this study about Jesus and the powerful qualities in His life that He wants in yours too. I think you can guess that this study starts with confidence, something Jessica—and you—needs a lot of. Confidence is a character quality that gave Jesus the courage to live out God's will during His time on earth. It gave Him the boldness to go through whatever God wanted Him to do. From Him you'll learn how to handle your challenges and fears—whether it involves your home life, your time at school, or just living like Jesus and being a witness for Him.

As you read, keep in mind the meaning of confidence. First of all, confidence begins with trust. Many people trust in their own abilities. These "self-made" people rely on their personalities, education, abilities, athletic skills, looks, health, and money. Their confidence in themselves makes them seem cool. It looks as if they have no problems. They don't appear to doubt themselves at all. They show no fear of embarrassment because they just know they will be successful. As long as they can trust in themselves, they believe there's nothing they can't accomplish.

But there's another kind of confidence—the best kind. It's also based on trust. However, it's not a trust in yourself, but a trust in God. The best example of the confidence that comes from trusting God is seen in God's only Son, the Lord Jesus. We first observe this character quality boldly lived out in Jesus at an early age.

Who Am I?

As you know all too well, preteen and teen years can be an extremely awkward age. Even torture! I know...and I remember. You want to grow up so badly, yet when you're given opportunities to accept more adult responsibilities, it's easy to want to retreat back into your safety zone. Your desire to be more grown-up and act like an adult is pushed aside by your fear of growing up and risking failure in new areas. Your fear of falling on your face is too strong.

But the young Jesus was different. Read about Him now and learn a lesson or two!

> *Every year his parents went to Jerusalem for the Feast of the Passover. When he was twelve years old, they went up to the Feast, according to the custom. After the Feast was over, while*

his parents were returning home, the boy Jesus stayed behind in Jerusalem, but they were unaware of it. Thinking he was in their company, they traveled on for a day. Then they began looking for him among their relatives and friends. When they did not find him, they went back to Jerusalem to look for him. After three days they found him in the temple courts, sitting among the teachers, listening to them and asking them questions. Everyone who heard him was amazed at his understanding and his answers. When his parents saw him, they were astonished. His mother said to him, "Son, why have you treated us like this? Your father and I have been anxiously searching for you." "Why were you searching for me?" he asked. "Didn't you know I had to be in my Father's house?" (Luke 2:41-49).

If you have a pencil, do a mini-Bible study by circling or underlining or writing out the who, what, where, and when of this story.

Who was Jesus traveling with?

What was the occasion?

Where did this incident occur?

When did it occur?

During this incident that occurred at the age of 12, Jesus' confidence became obvious to Mary (His mother) and Joseph. When His mother questioned Him after finding Him in the temple courts, Jesus was surprised she didn't understand why He was doing what He was doing, and that she had forgotten His role as the Son of God. After all, the angel Gabriel had communicated to Mary exactly who her baby was (Luke 1:30-33). At the early age of 12, Jesus had a clear awareness of His identity. He already showed bold confidence in His mission. And He was already busy preparing to do the special work the Father had for Him.

A question for your heart: Like the Lord's confidence in His Father, your confidence must come from your identity in and with Jesus as your Savior. He has made you a new creation (2 Corinthians 5:17) and given you a fresh start. Your past has been forgiven. The slate of your sins has been erased. You now have the power of Jesus' Spirit. And your future is guaranteed for all eternity. You are one with Christ. Therefore you have no need to be fearful of anything.

Oh, you should have a healthy respect for the fragility of life and the need for wisdom and safety. And you'll always need to do your part when it comes to responsibilities (like taking your class report seriously!). But there's no reason to be anxious about your everyday activities. Just remember that confidence is based on trust. If your confidence for some challenge is wavering, maybe you've lost sight of who you are to trust. Trusting in yourself is shaky ground. Trust instead in the rock that is solid, in Jesus Christ.

Now the question is this: Have you put your trust in Jesus, God's Son, who died for your sins? Answer from your heart. If you belong to Christ, thank God and live for Him with confidence. If the answer is *no* or you aren't sure, we'll be talking more about knowing Jesus as Savior as we go through this book. Ask God to make His plan of salvation clear to you as you seek Him with all your heart.

Life Is Scary!

In another scene in the Bible, Jesus prayed all night and then chose 12 disciples to follow Him and be trained for future ministry (Matthew 10:16-26). Before sending them out to do ministry work, Jesus cautioned them, explaining, "I am sending you out like sheep among wolves" (verse 16). He then ran through a list of all sorts of horrible things that might happen to them as they served in His name. They would even be accused of working for Satan (verses 17-26)!

This doesn't seem like a very good way to boost the confidence level of a new team, does it? A talk like that would be enough to make most people quit before they even began! But Jesus wanted to give His disciples a true picture of what they would face. He told them the truth. He prepared them and made them wiser about what was really out there. It was a sobering heads-up speech.

But Jesus wasn't finished. On the heels of the negative came the positive. To ensure that their confidence wouldn't waver, He ended His pep talk with the promise of God's care. He told the disciples that the same God who takes care of the unimportant little sparrow would surely take care of them. Then He said, "So don't be afraid; you are worth more than many sparrows" (Matthew 10:31).

Think about it! God places great value on you. In fact, you are so valuable that He sent His only Son to die for you (John 3:16). And because of God's love, you never need to be afraid of personal threats or difficult trials—or the mean girls at school. This should cause you to have a different view of your life. Yes, times of trouble will come, but instead of cowering in fear, remember Jesus' words, "Don't be afraid." Have the confidence to trust your loving heavenly Father. Yes, the wolves are out there. But the Good Shepherd knows that you are one of His sheep. He is always there with you and for you.

A question for your heart: How do you view yourself? As unimportant? As someone who hasn't found her niche? As nothing very special? As a loser? Look at the following verses and note what you should be thinking about yourself.

> *God so loved the world that he gave his one and only Son* (John 3:16).

> *I am fearfully and wonderfully made* (Psalm 139:14).

He [God] made us accepted in the Beloved [Jesus]
(Ephesians 1:6 NKJV).

Where Is Your Confidence Now?

Here's a key fact about the 12 disciples-in-training: They
were confident only as long as they were in Jesus' presence. But during their last supper together, when Jesus told
them that He was leaving, they were shaken to the core.
Their confidence fell to an all-time low. This is what Jesus
said to instruct His troubled disciples not to worry. Be sure
to underline what you need to remember the next time you
are worried or afraid.

> *Do not let your hearts be troubled. Trust in God;*
> *trust also in me* (John 14:1).

And a few days later, the disciples' confidence returned
after Jesus rose from the grave and after the Holy Spirit
came upon them. Amazingly, from that point onward,
these men who had been so afraid "spoke the word of
God boldly" (Acts 4:31). They went on to become men who
"turned the world upside down" for Jesus (17:6 NKJV).

What happened? The disciples finally realized that their
trust had to be in Jesus, not themselves. If Jesus is your
Savior, then you too have hope for the future. Whatever
might happen in the days to come, it doesn't really matter.
Why? Because you have placed your trust in a strong and
mighty Savior who has promised to strengthen you all the

days of your life. He has already given you all His great and precious promises and everything you need to live for Him (2 Peter 1:3-4). You are indeed blessed!

How to Handle Tough Times

Jesus showed total resolve and confidence every day of His earthly ministry. He put up with constant accusations and mistreatment from the religious leaders in Israel. He ministered to those who sought Him out and crossed His path. Yet He never hesitated in His forward movement toward the cross.

On the night before His betrayal, trial, crucifixion, and death, Jesus fought His own battle with following through on God's plan for Him. How did He fight and win this battle? He prayed, "Father, if you are willing, take this cup from me; yet not my will, but yours be done" (Luke 22:42).

Before you move on, jot down the answers to a few quick questions:

> What did Jesus do when He struggled to follow God's will?

> What did Jesus first ask the Father?

What was the desire of Jesus' heart?

The conflict was over and the battle was won! The confidence Jesus was seeking was there. After praying and talking with God, all was settled.

Like Jesus, you will have times when you have a difficult decision to make or something hard to do. During these times of crisis, follow Jesus' example. Pray! Take your questions and fears to the Father. Ask Him for the confidence you need to do what's right in spite of your fears and doubts. And most of all, tell God that your greatest desire is to do His will, not yours. God will be honored and you will be blessed when you trust Him and do His will with full confidence.

Meet Your Number One Helper

The disciples often struggled with confidence. Perhaps their all-time low was when they fled in fear after Jesus was arrested. Later they came back and gathered around Jesus after He rose from the dead. But they were still hesitant and fearful, even to the time of Jesus' return to heaven. So, as a final confidence booster, Jesus made one last promise to the disciples before ascending into heaven. He promised, "You will receive power when the Holy Spirit comes on you; and you will be my witnesses in Jerusalem, and in all Judea and Samaria, and to the ends of the earth" (Acts 1:8).

When this promise of the Holy Spirit came true, the unsure disciples were completely transformed! They boldly preached the good news of Jesus, and thousands believed. This threatened the religious leaders so much that they rounded up the disciples and questioned them. They were looking for some kind of explanation for the new power and confidence the disciples suddenly possessed. And what happened? "When they saw the courage of Peter and John and realized that they were unschooled, ordinary men, they were astonished and they took note that these men had been with Jesus" (Acts 4:13).

What do you learn here about boldness and confidence?

How are Peter and John described (and do you ever feel like that)?

What was the only explanation for Peter and John's confidence and impact on others?

We know what made a difference in the attitudes of the

disciples, don't we? They went from being cowards to confident spokesmen for Christ. How did this happen? They had received the power of the Holy Spirit. It was the Spirit's confidence that empowered them. "After they prayed, the place where they were meeting was shaken. And they were all filled with the Holy Spirit and spoke the word of God boldly" (Acts 4:31).

The apostle Paul also realized the source of his confidence as he preached Christ with boldness. Here's how he explained it: "I came to you in weakness and fear, and with much trembling. My message and my preaching were not with wise and persuasive words, but with a demonstration of the Holy Spirit's power" (1 Corinthians 2:4).

How does Paul describe himself (and have you ever felt like this)?

How does he describe his preaching?

How does he explain the impact his preaching made?

Paul's confidence was not in his keen intellect or speaking ability. No, instead, his confidence was in the Holy Spirit. He knew the Spirit was working in the hearts of those who listened and, at the same time, was empowering and guiding him as he obeyed God and did what God asked him to do.

Reflecting the Heart of Jesus

Confidence. It's a quality everyone desires and anyone can possess. Yet amazingly, few have it! You can take classes or receive special training to help you become more self-assured and bold. Anyone can become more confident. But the confidence that comes from Jesus is based on trust—trust in Him alone.

Here's something to reflect on, to think about: When things are new or scary, where do you usually place your trust? In Jesus...or in yourself? In general, is your confidence going steadily up as you count on Christ to help you, or have you forgotten to look to Jesus for strength and assurance? When you remember to look to Jesus, lean on Him, and do His will, there is no reason for self-doubt or timidity.

Make a goal of taking your eyes off of yourself and off of the challenge in front of you and redirecting your focus onto Jesus. It's true that you can have confidence in Him. You can trust in His power to assist you through whatever is ahead and whatever is required of you. He is all you need for a bold confident life. Why? Because, as He explained to His disciples after His resurrection, "All authority in heaven and on earth has been given to me" (Matthew 28:18). Therefore go forward into the wonderful life that is in front of you with confidence—confidence in Jesus. He'll be right there beside you all the way.

∽ A Prayer to Pray ∽

Thank You, Lord Jesus, that You give me the power I need to do what You want me to do and be what You want me to be. Thank You that I can have confidence in everything that I do because You are with me. I'm so glad that You know every step I will take and You will help me, no matter what I face. Great are You, Lord, and greatly to be praised! Amen.

Want to Know More About... Being Confident?

Share what these verses say about confidence and its source. Write out the parts of the verses that instruct you about how to be more confident and the source of your confidence.

Psalm 23:4—

Psalm 56:3—

Psalm 56:4—

1 Corinthians 2:4—

Ephesians 2:10—

Ephesians 3:20—

Philippians 4:13—

Which of these verses were your favorites or the most challenging, and why?

2

Faithful

Faithful Is as Faithful Does

As Jessica sat on her bed staring off into space, she couldn't believe the mess she was in. "How many projects, teams, and commitments can one girl get into?!" As she tried to solve her problem of too many activities—and too little time for schoolwork—she found herself asking, "Now, let me see... who don't I want to disappoint? Will it be Bob, Jennifer, and Randy in my science project group? (There's just no way I can get my part done before the project is due!) Or will it be the members of my swim team? (Never mind I'm the anchor for the medley race and the meet is in two weeks!)"

And then there were her poor parents. Jessica had tried to follow through on her commitment to take more interest in her family and spend more time with them. But she knew she had really blown it when she came up with an excuse for not going with her parents to see her Uncle Brad, who had just found out he had cancer.

Now here she was, face-to-face with her failures in her schoolwork and her after-school participation in the swim team. And, of course, the fact she had disappointed her family.

Well, just maybe, Jessica thought, *there might be something in this week's lesson on Jesus that will help.* In fact, Jessica even surprised herself when a prayer leaped out of her heart—"Lord, please give me some help tonight!"

Again, just like last week, Jessica was about to get another dose of Jesus! And yet even though she had taken one step forward and two steps back, she was beginning to reflect Jesus a little bit more in her life.

And God knew what Jessica needed, for this week's lesson would definitely help her—and you!—look more to Jesus and learn about His faithfulness.

Jesus Shows You the Way

No matter what area you struggle in or what character quality falls into your "Needs Improvement" category, Jesus gloriously shows you the way to victory. Yes, He was God-in-flesh. And yes, He was perfect. But He was also fully man, and as man, He struggled with temptation and prayed to His Father that He would be faithful to do the Father's will. With your favorite pen or pencil in hand, read Hebrews 4:15.

> *We do not have a high priest who is unable to sympathize with our weaknesses, but we have one who has been tempted in every way, just as we are—yet was without sin.*

If you are able, jot down three things you learn about Jesus from this verse. Just copy the words from the verse for each truth.

—His ability to relate to your struggles:

—His experience with every kind of temptation:

—His condition in spite of temptation:

And there's more to learn. Take a minute to read verse 16 (see below) several times:

Let us then approach the throne of grace with confidence, so that we may receive mercy and find grace to help us in our time of need.

—What are you to do when you are tempted or need help?

—When are you to do it?

—What will the result be?

Dealing with Peer Pressure

Jesus was faithful to God's purpose, no matter what... and no matter what others thought. He came to earth for a purpose. As you read John 4:34 below, underline the two purposes mentioned in it.

> *My food...is to do the will of him who sent me and to finish his work.*

Jesus' purpose was to live and die as the perfect sacrifice for people's sin. But as Jesus went about doing good and feeding the multitudes, the number of those who followed Him exploded. Soon it was evident His followers had a different purpose for Jesus, especially after they witnessed Him feeding thousands and thousands of people. They wanted Him to be their leader and to provide food for them on a regular basis.

But no matter what the people wanted or asked for, Jesus stayed on track. He was faithful to His purpose. He told the crowds, "I have come down from heaven not to do my will [or, by the way, your will either] but to do the will of him who sent me" (John 6:38).

To the very end, day by day Jesus faithfully moved toward the objective that God set for Him. It was His faithfulness that made it possible for Him to state in prayer on the eve of His death, "I have brought you glory on earth by completing the work you gave me to do" (John 17:4).

I don't know about you, but it's really easy to get sidetracked on the way to doing what God calls us to do with our lives. This person wants me to do this, and another wants me to do that. I'm pulled in all different directions. And then there are those days I'm not sure I really want to do *any*thing! Do you ever feel like this? Well, maybe the reason for the distractions and confusion is that we don't know our true purpose in life...or haven't reviewed it in a while. Then we find ourselves trying to ride off in all directions at once...or just doing nothing!

What does God want you and me to do with our lives? I've been learning from the Bible what God wants from me. It's different for me than it is for you because I'm married and have children, and believe me, God's Word is very clear about exactly what that means for me!

But God speaks just as clearly to you at your wonderful

age. As a teen girl, you can know that His will for you includes:

- Loving God with all your heart—*Love the Lord your God with all your heart and with all your soul and with all your mind* (Matthew 22:37).

- Loving others, including your brothers and sisters—*Love each other* (John 15:12).

- Loving and obeying Jesus by keeping His commandments—*If you love me, you will obey what I command* (John 14:15).

- Obeying your parents—*Children, obey your parents* (Ephesians 6:1-2).

- Telling others about Him—*You will be my witnesses* (Acts 1:8).

- Doing all things for Jesus—*Whatever you do, work at it with all your heart, as working for the Lord* (Colossians 3:23).

- Growing in the Lord and more like Jesus—*Grow in the grace and knowledge of our Lord and Savior Jesus Christ* (2 Peter 3:18).

Why not put a checkmark beside the one you need to work on right away?

A question for your heart: Hopefully you are already pursuing God's goals for you and seeking to be more like Jesus. As a follow-up you might also want to ask yourself,

"Am I willing to follow in Jesus' steps of faithfulness? Am I listening to Him and not to 'them'—to all the voices of my friends, peers, popular people, TV, magazines, words in music—and what they are telling me to do?" Growing more like Jesus is right on the other side of these answers and actions.

What's the Big Deal About Prayer?

Jesus was also faithful in prayer. One of the most amazing aspects of Jesus coming as a man is the fact that He chose to submit Himself to the control of the Holy Spirit. Prayer was a key way Jesus communicated with the Father and received direction. Jesus lived in the spirit of prayer. Through prayer He could be alone with the Father in the middle of a pressing crowd or in a secluded place. Prayer was His life, His habit. He prayed in every situation, in every emergency, and at every opportunity for all issues. For instance,

> He prayed in the midst of a busy life. Most people stress out under the pressure of too much activity. But not our Lord. He had another way of dealing with the pressure of one hectic day after another. What was His secret? After perhaps the busiest day of His ministry, we see that the next day, "very early in the morning, while it was still dark, Jesus got up, left the house and went off to a solitary place, where he prayed" (Mark 1:35).

> He prayed before and during important events, particularly His impending death on the cross (Matthew 26:39-42).

He prayed for others. Intercession for others was a dominant feature in His prayers. (Read through Jesus' High Priestly Prayer in John 17 during your devotions.)

He prayed for His enemies. "Father, forgive them, for they do not know what they are doing" (Luke 23:34).

You cannot read very far in the Gospels without sensing the importance of prayer in the life of Jesus. He repeatedly taught all who listened that "they should always pray and not give up" (Luke 18:1). His commitment to faithful prayer is calling you to diligently and seriously develop the habit of prayer. Jot down one thing right here, right now, that you will do to enjoy the blessings of prayer.

Faithfulness Starts with Family and Friends

Jesus was faithful to His family, friends, and disciples too. Loyalty is a rare quality whether today or in Jesus' day. Jesus had parents, numerous siblings, friends, and, of course, His 12 disciples. He enjoyed time with them, taught them, provided for them, protected them, cared for them, and loved them.

JESUS' FAMILY

Jesus was faithful to His family. He did not begin His ministry until He was about 30 years old (Luke 3:23). Can you imagine how patient Jesus, God in flesh, had to be to wait until He was 30? A Jewish boy was considered a man at about age 12. So what was Jesus doing during all those years of waiting? The Bible doesn't say, but as the oldest son, it would have been Jesus' responsibility to care for the family if or when Joseph died. Jesus probably faithfully cared for His mother and half brothers and half sisters until some of the boys were old enough to assist in the support of the family.

Jesus said to "honor your father and mother" (Matthew 15:4). And He lived out such honor when "he went down to Nazareth with them and was obedient to them" after reminding them (at age 12) of who He was and His mission from God (Luke 2:51).

To the very end of His life, Jesus did not abandon Mary, His mother. And He modeled how honor is fleshed out. In the last hours of His life, Jesus showed you how important parents are. Looking down from the cross upon His mother and His disciple John, Jesus said, "'Dear woman, here is your son,' and to the disciple, 'Here is your mother.' From that time on, this disciple took her into his home" (John 19:26-27).

Jesus showed love and respect for His mother by faithfully placing her into the care of John. And you are to do the same. You are to see your family as important, not only your parents and stepparents, but also your brothers and sisters.

JESUS' FRIENDS

Other than His disciples, Jesus had few people close enough to Him to be considered friends. On one occasion

He received a report that Lazarus, whom He called "friend" in John 11:11, was sick. In spite of death threats made against His life if He ever returned to Lazarus's hometown, Jesus faithfully traveled to minister to His friend. Braving death Himself, Jesus went to Lazarus as a friend. What love! As Jesus said in John 15:13, "Greater love hath no man than this, that a man lay down his life for his friends" (KJV).

JESUS' DISCIPLES

With "the Twelve," Jesus again modeled the quality of faithfulness. He acknowledged that they were special because the Father had given them to Him, and He was in charge of them and responsible for them. To God He referred to this group as "those whom you gave me out of the world. They were yours; you gave them to me" (John 17:6). Jesus also reported to God, "While I was with them, I protected them and kept them safe by that name you gave me" (John 17:12).

A question for your heart: Do you realize that God has given you your family members and friends? And He asks for your faithfulness with these precious lives—to love them, appreciate them, and help them. As a saying goes, In the final analysis God will not evaluate your life based on how successful you've been but on how faithful you've been in taking care of the people and things He put in your life. Galatians 5:22 tells us faithfulness is a fruit of the Holy Spirit, who lives in you. That means when you are faithful to the people in your life, to God's goals, and to do your work, you are reflecting Jesus!

Faithful in All Things

As I began growing as a Christian woman, I ran across a life-changing verse in 1 Timothy 3:11. Simply stated, the verse said women are to be faithful in everything they do. Until I read that verse, I pretty much did whatever I wanted to do, and I didn't do what I didn't want to do. But once I met up with this truth from God, I knew I had to get serious about being who God wanted me to be (a faithful servant) and doing what God wanted me to do (be faithful in all things).

Since then I've taken on a few mottos that really help me, and I'm thinking they will help you too. And, you guessed it—they are right out of the Bible.

—Whatever you do, do well (see Ecclesiastes 9:10).

—Work brings profit; talk brings poverty (see Proverbs 14:23).

—Work hard and cheerfully at all you do (or have to do!), just as though you were working for the Lord (see Colossians 3:23).

—Do everything for the glory of God, even your eating and drinking (see 1 Corinthians 10:31).

Hopefully by now you are getting a better understanding of how faithful Jesus was. He was faithful to finish the work the Father gave Him—to die on the cross for you. And He will be faithful to fulfill all His promises to you. And now He is asking you to be faithful too, to be faithful in everything you do. Faithfulness is a powerful character quality, one that definitely, without any doubt, beautifully reflects Jesus in your life.

Reflecting the Heart of Jesus

As a Christian woman, it is vital that faithfulness be a quality that shines brilliantly in you. Why? Because your faithfulness—a quality in Christ—will reflect Jesus to others. When you're faithful, you show that you are born of God and belong to Him. Jesus had a heart for the Father and doing His will. He had a heart for others and praying for them. And He had a heart for family and caring for them.

As you walk in faithfulness, you will mirror the heart of your faithful Savior. Your faithfulness will bear fruit in the lives of those you come in contact with. Your family will be blessed because of your faithful help, love, and loyalty. Your church will benefit from your faithful service. And if you hold down a job, your boss and fellow employees will profit from your faithfulness.

We've marveled at many instances of Jesus' faithfulness. And the good news is you can develop this same sterling quality. You can grow in faithfulness that follows through, delivers the goods, shows up, keeps her word and her commitments, and is devoted to duty. And if this sounds impossible or like a hard uphill road, take courage! Step one? Call upon God in prayer. And start small...in the little things. Count on Jesus' strength too. In Him you can do all things, including be faithful (see Philippians 4:13). And ask God for His enabling grace to work at eliminating laziness and fulfilling one of His purposes for you—that you would be "faithful in all things" (1 Timothy 3:11 NASB).

Our great, faithful God has already faithfully given you everything you need so you can be faithful. He has given you a "Helper" in the Holy Spirit. He has given you His

Word, the Bible, to serve as your guide. And, praise upon praise, He's given you Jesus as a living model of faithfulness. Jesus lived out faithfulness day by day, minute by minute, incident by incident—and you can too. In our Savior's words, "Whoever can be trusted with very little can also be trusted with much" (Luke 16:10). Once again, start small, for faithfulness in a little thing is a great thing.

A Prayer to Pray

Lord Jesus, may I day by day walk by Your Spirit so faithfulness is reflected in my life. May I stand before You when my days on earth are done and hear You say, "Well done, good and faithful servant." This, dear Jesus, is my heart's desire. Amen.

Want to Know More About...
Being Faithful?

To begin, what does Lamentations 3:22-23 say about God's faithfulness?

Now scan through Proverbs 31:10-31. How did this woman show faithfulness in her daily life, according to these verses?

Verses 11-13—

Verses 14-15—

Verses 18-19—

Verse 20—

Verses 21-22 and 24—

Verse 26—

Verse 27—

Verse 30—

Which of these verses were your favorites or the most challenging, and why?

3

★ ★ ★ ★

Focused

Keep Your Eye on the Ball

 "Jessica, what do you want to be when you grow up?"

"Jessica, you have great potential! Why are you wasting your life on things that don't matter?"

"Jessica, if you would apply yourself, you could be a good student!"

"Jessica, wake up! Where is your life heading? Don't you have any goals?"

"Jessica, you could be a great swimmer if you would just focus your energies."

These were only a few of the questions and comments that had been thrown at Jessica from her teachers, church leaders, piano teachers, swim coaches, and a long list of others for what seemed like forever!

And, of course, Jessica's favorite came from her parents: "Jessica, what's wrong with you? Your older sister, Ruth, knew exactly what she wanted to do with her life way before she was your age. What's the matter with you?"

By now, Jessica was numb from all the comments. She just wished people would get off her back. *Maybe if I make something up, they'll leave me alone,* she thought. *After all,* she rationalized, *I'm only a junior in high school. How can anyone know what they want to do with their life at my age? I've got years left to make those kinds of decisions. And besides, I like going with the flow. I like, you know, just drifting along. It's definitely less threatening if I don't have any goals. At least that means I won't fail at something else!*

Jessica is not alone in her "going with the flow" lifestyle. Many girls her age and older are drifting through life, not knowing for sure what to do with their time or themselves. Yet by taking this approach, they lose precious years of opportunities for growth and training that would prepare them for a future of blessing, both in their own lives and the lives of others.

Well, Jessica was in for another jolt as she aimlessly drifted into the youth center. God was about to rock her "boat of complacency" as she encountered her next lesson from the life of Jesus—a lesson about focus.

Jesus Shows You the Way

"Aim at nothing and you will hit it every time." Have you heard that quip before? Well, aimlessness is what living without focus produces. You wake up each day and head off in all directions at once—or in no direction at all! But today we get a chance to pause and gaze at the quality of "focus" in Jesus' life. We're treated to a look at our Lord and how He focused and lived according to purpose. He showed us the way to live by a handful of practices. Five key features marked His days. They propelled Jesus toward fulfilling His mission, and they can help you too.

Get Ready and Get Set!

KEY #1: JESUS PREPARED

One of my favorite quotes for daily living and purpose is this: "Success is when preparation meets opportunity." Preparation is a necessary step in living out God's plans and purposes for you. It helps you to seize opportunities as they show up in your day, or in life. But be careful. As the famous inventor Thomas Edison said, "Opportunity is missed by most people because it looks like work."[1]

And, of course, Jesus is the ultimate illustration of this. He spent almost 30 years preparing for the day when He began His ministry. The same was true of Jesus' cousin, John the Baptist, who also spent 30 years preparing for his one-year ministry of announcing the coming of Messiah. These two men's paths crossed at the Jordan River, where John was baptizing people and Jesus showed up to be baptized. Immediately after His baptism, Jesus began His three years of earthly ministry. As the Bible reports, "Jesus himself was about thirty years old when he began his ministry" (Luke 3:23).

Yes, Jesus began His ministry at age 30. But He didn't wait until He was 30 years old to prepare for the work God had given Him to do. He prepared for it for three decades. And He didn't wait 30 years to bless and serve others because we know He served His family at home as He was growing up. And you and I shouldn't wait to serve others either. While we're gaining knowledge and skills and growing in faith, we can serve in a multitude of ways. For you, that would include serving your parents and, yes, your brothers and sisters as well!

I know you already have a lot of responsibilities. There's your schoolwork, and you already take part in your family's activities. And maybe you babysit or have a part-time job. And you probably have after-school activities galore. And then there are your friends! But you can still set apart some of your time to learn something that moves you toward a special goal.

For example, in my own life I spent bits and pieces of time each day over a period of seven years learning about the women in the Bible. Like you, I had a long list of responsibilities…and I still do. But I needed and wanted to grow as a Christian and as a Christian woman. And I needed lessons in trusting God and following Him in faith. Then one day an "opportunity" came through a letter in the mailbox. I was invited to teach a workshop on the women of the Bible to a small group of ladies. I prayed and then hesitantly said *yes*. Well, the short story is that I continued to teach, and for 20-plus years I taught a variety of women's Bible studies at my church. And in God's timing, that teaching ministry developed into a writing ministry.

Now, I want to quickly say that's what has happened in my own life. God's direction for every person is different. I'm not saying you should set a goal to become a teacher. No, my point is for you to prepare yourself for whatever God might want to do through you. As you read the Bible, grow spiritually, and seek God's direction through prayer, and as you serve God's people in any way you can, opportunities will come your way. Maybe you'll have a friend who needs guidance and you'll surprise yourself as you give her wise advice. Or maybe you'll be asked to organize some activity at church or to join or lead a committee. Or maybe you'll volunteer to help an elderly person in your church or neighborhood. Or maybe you'll sign up to help with the toddlers at church on Sundays.

Who knows what you'll want to do or get to do? As the Bible says, "There are different kinds of gifts...different kinds of service...different kinds of working" or activities (1 Corinthians 12:4-6). As you prepare yourself and grow spiritually, you'll be preparing yourself for a future contribution and great joy.

A question for your heart: To live with purpose means to focus and take advantage of each day, not only to help others, but to prepare yourself for the future. Then when amazing opportunities present themselves, you'll be ready. What can you do today to prepare for the opportunities that are waiting just around the corner? Could you jot down a few goals? Read your Bible? Go to the library and check out a book about something you're interested in? Talk to someone who's doing something you'd like to know how to do? If your pen is ready, list at least three small steps you can take today.

—

—

—

Before you begin this next section, note several things you learn about Jesus from this verse:

> *When all the people were being baptized, Jesus was baptized too. And as he was praying, heaven was opened* (Luke 3:21).

KEY #2: JESUS PRAYED

At the beginning of (and throughout) His ministry, Jesus prayed. After 30 years of preparation, Jesus launched His ministry by first being baptized, and as that was happening, He prayed. I'm sure you noticed that in the verse above.

You'll hear many times in this book about how important prayer is. It's vital! And you'll see it modeled by Jesus again and again. He was in constant fellowship with the Father. As you move through this book, you'll see Him praying before events (like before He chose the 12 disciples), praying at events (for instance, at the Last Supper), and praying for an upcoming event (as He did before His trial and death.)[2]

A question for your heart: Is God's purpose for you firmly fixed in your mind yet? Be sure to look to Jesus and allow Him to be your perfect model. He knew God's plan, focused on it, prepared for it, and lived it out. As you steadily make prayer a habit, you'll discover God's purpose for you at this time in your life as He leads you. Take prayer seriously. Keep checking in with God. Keep asking Him to give you ideas and opportunities. You'll enjoy the thrill of anticipation each day as you pray and see God unfolding the wonderful life that awaits you.

KEY #3: JESUS PLANNED

What was His plan? Read the verses below and then answer that question. If possible, mark or list several plans Jesus had in mind for you.

> *He chose us in him before the creation of the world to be holy and blameless in his sight. In love he predestined us to be adopted as his sons through Jesus Christ, in accordance with his pleasure and will* (Ephesians 1:4-5).

What is your favorite truth in these verses, and why?

It's obvious that you and I benefitted from God's plan! Aren't you glad there was a plan? And you need to plan too so you are growing spiritually and practically. Here's a tip—making a daily schedule helps. Your schedule is a plan. When you have a plan for your day it helps you to break your goals and dreams down into small bits and pieces that you can easily accomplish. Aim at completing the "bite-sized" pieces, and you'll find yourself making better progress in all that you do.

So take a few minutes each day to make a schedule. How hard is that? Surely there's something of lesser value you can give up for a few minutes so that you can plan your time, your day, and the pursuit of your dreams. All it takes is skipping a couple of text messages or a phone call or using the commercial time during a favorite TV program. Just come up with one or two steps you can take toward your goals. Like finding a book that will help you develop yourself or some skill. Like picking a song for a solo to work on. Or setting a time to practice a musical instrument. I'm sure you're getting the picture!

With a plan and a schedule in your hand and your heart, pray! Give your plan to God. Ask Him to help you focus on the activities you planned so you can grow.

Now you're ready to proceed!

Get Ready, Get Set…and Go!

We've discussed goals, purposes, preparing, planning, scheduling, and praying. Now try to find these elements in the following verses. I hope your pen is handy!

As the time approached for him to be taken up

to heaven, Jesus resolutely set out for Jerusalem (Luke 9:51). (Just a note: Jerusalem is where Jesus died on the cross.)

—Jesus' goal:

—Jesus' timetable:

—Jesus' purposefulness or determination:

The Son of Man did not come to be served, but to serve, and to give his life as a ransom for many (Matthew 20:28).

—Jesus' goals:

—Jesus' purpose:

KEY #4: JESUS PROCEEDED

We can make plans all day long, but until we move out in action to make those plans a reality, it's just talk. The day finally arrived when Jesus knew that His time on earth was just about over. The time was coming for His death and His return to heaven. Therefore it was time to proceed and fulfill the purpose of His coming to earth. Jesus knew He would be humiliated and face death when He got to Jerusalem. But He was determined to go there, no matter what. Knowing His purpose gave Jesus strength to complete the joyous but difficult task that had been given to Him by the Father.

A question for your heart: Focus and preparation are key to doing God's will. Jesus was determined to proceed to Jerusalem in spite of what He knew was waiting for Him. That's the kind of resolve that can characterize your life too. So...how would you rate your level of focus and determination? Are you easily distracted from growing spiritually and living for God? Do you have goals in mind, goals you are moving toward? Distraction comes easily when a plan isn't clearly fixed in your mind. Hopefully you have a plan firmly set in your mind and are steadily proceeding toward fulfilling God's purpose.

Trust God

KEY #5: GOD PROVIDED

Once you focus yourself on goals that are worthwhile, and you plan and prepare for those goals, you'll be surprised by the many ways God provides for you. God's purpose for both Jesus' life and yours includes His provision in at least two areas.

First, the Father promises to help us when we are tempted. Now, because Jesus was God, He couldn't sin. But the Bible tells us that He was tempted just like we are (Hebrews 4:15). That means Jesus understands the struggles you face. Amazingly, during several of the times Jesus was tempted, the Father provided angels to minister to Jesus because He was under extreme physical stress.

On one occasion, Jesus was tested and tempted by Satan for 40 days while Jesus had no food. What happened? As you read, note and underline how God took care of His Son as He was tempted.

> *He was in the desert forty days, being tempted by Satan. He was with the wild animals, and angels attended him* (Mark 1:13).

Another time occurred in the garden of Gethsemane when Jesus was facing death. There Jesus wrestled in prayer with His purpose. During His time of agony in prayer,

> *an angel from heaven appeared to him and strengthened him. And being in anguish, he prayed more earnestly, and his sweat was like drops of blood falling to the ground* (Luke 22:43-44).

In the midst of these two temptations to lose heart and stop trusting in the Father, the Father provided for His Son. Angels were sent to minister to Jesus, protect Him, and strengthen Him.

Now, don't start looking for angels! But do keep believing in God. Do keep trusting Him to strengthen you and provide for all your needs. He will help you when you are tempted. And He will help you when you think you are at your limits. He has great and exciting plans for you. And He also knows sin can hinder the fulfillment of those plans. So, as the apostle Paul explains,

> *God is faithful; he will not let you be tempted beyond what you can bear. But when you are tempted, he will also provide a way out so that you can stand up under it* (1 Corinthians 10:13).

How is God described here?

In your own words, what is God's promise to you when you are tempted?

A question for your heart: God is faithful. Let this truth refresh your heart. God will not always remove your temptations because they make your faith in Him stronger as you resist. However, He does promise to keep the temptation from becoming so strong that you can't stand up under it. Whatever you do, don't try to deal with your temptations alone. Through prayer, the help of God's Word, and support from others, God is faithful to provide the way for you so you can remain faithful to Him when you are tempted.

And second, the Father provides for all life's needs. The apostle Paul wrote, "God will meet all your needs according to his glorious riches in Christ Jesus" (Philippians 4:19). If Jesus is your personal Savior, you, along with all believers, have this promise of provision for all your real needs. You can always count on God to supply all that you need to live for Him and do His will.

Think about it. God has provided for all your needs. What a magnificent promise! He has a purpose for you. And you can move toward fulfilling it without fear or anxiety because of His guaranteed 100 percent provision. Whatever your need is today, whether it's something in your family; something at school; something physical, financial, emotional, or spiritual; you can boldly take that need to God. Then watch as the Father helps you fulfill your purpose by supplying all your needs according to His riches in glory by and because of His Son, Jesus.

Reflecting the Heart of Jesus

When I think of Jesus, the first thought that comes to my mind in this area of focus and purpose and usefulness is that Jesus was *busy*. I don't mean busy like you and I are usually busy, as in too busy, always rushing off somewhere to do anything and everything. No, I mean that Jesus stayed busy. He didn't sit around. He didn't mope around. He didn't get bored. He wasn't lazy. He just kept moving among the people and helping them. Because He had prepared, He had things to give to people. Wisdom. Compassion. An understanding of the Word and knowledge of God. He fed them, ministered to their needs, touched them, healed them, encouraged them, taught them, and loved them.

Another thought I have about Jesus is He was *prayerful*. He always had time to pray. And He checked in with God in the morning and talked through His day and His life with His heavenly Father. As you probably know from your own experience with prayer, when you've done this, you rise up from prayer with power—God's power—for the day ahead. You rise up with confidence because you have direction and a plan.

Jesus was also *unselfish*. He was never self-centered. He was not the needy one having to make everyone else join in and listen to His problems and issues and complaints. No, He had met with God and had His own heart ministered to by the Father and was ready to focus fully on the needs of others.

And Jesus was *calm*. He wasn't frazzled by His responsibilities. He never had a panic attack. He didn't pace back and forth and wring His hands. There was a rock-like calm as He went through each day living out His purpose and moving quietly—steadfastly—toward the cross. He knew His purpose. He knew the goal of His life. He knew why He came to this earth and where He was going. He knew He had been planning and preparing for it and that He was living it.

It's very liberating when you know your purpose in life. To drift aimlessly through each day is tiresome and unrewarding—even dull and boring. It would be a great tragedy to wake up one day and realize all you could have accomplished if you had focused on some goals along the way. You may already know your purpose for now. If so, focus your time and energies on it. But if you're a little behind or uncertain, spend time looking at Jesus' life and thinking about how He spent His time and energy. Pay close attention to His focus and confidence as He lived God's purpose day by day. Notice how He fixed His gaze on God's plan for Him. And then do the same. Then you'll truly reflect Jesus in your life!

∽ A Prayer to Pray ∽

Blessed Jesus, I have so many options each day for how I spend my time and where I put my focus. And I admit it's easy to be lazy. But my heart wants to live for You and live out Your plan for me. Please lead the way. Make it clear to me. I want to follow! Amen.

Want to Know More About...
Staying Focused?

Read the verses mentioned here in your Bible, and then answer the questions.

Prepare

2 Timothy 2:15—List several areas in which you need to be more disciplined in preparing for your future.

Pray

Philippians 4:6-7—Underline the four different terms used here to refer to prayer, and write them below.

As you focus on your future, share several ways prayer will help you with fear and worry.

Plan

Proverbs 16:3—What does the wise young woman do?

And what does the foolish young woman do?

Proverbs 16:9—What is your role in focusing on your day or your future?

And what is God's role?

Proceed

Philippians 3:13-14—List the three steps you can take to reach God's goal for you.

Provision

Psalm 23:1—What is God's promise to you and His people?

Psalm 34:10—What is the secret to enjoying God's provision?

Philippians 4:19—Again, what is God's promise to you and His people?

Place a star or check mark next to the verse or verses that encouraged you the most. Which one will you memorize?

4

★ ★ ★ ★

Friendly

Everyone Needs a Friend

 As usual, Jessica was sitting alone in the school cafeteria during lunch. Recently she had been telling herself that it didn't matter if she had friends or not. In fact, a so-called—and now ex—"friend" had passed on gossip to others about Jessica's feelings about a certain boy in one of her classes. How embarrassing was that? *Nope,* Jessica thought, *I'm never going to let anyone get that close to me again!*

Day after day, Jessica sat alone, determined not to reach out, resolved not to even *try* to make friends with anyone ever again. She wasn't in the "cool crowd," so there was no hope for making friends there. And she wasn't part of the "bizarre bunch" who dressed and acted like they were from some weird alien planet. In fact, Jessica concluded, "I'm not even a candidate for *any* group!" She tried to hide her pain, but her heart was breaking as she relived over and over again what someone she thought was a true friend had done to her. "Just when I thought I was finally going to have at least one friend!"

Now, quickly flash forward to Jessica's evening. It's youth night at church where, once again, she's sitting alone, only this time in the back row of the youth classroom at church. Little does she know that all her turmoil about friends and friendships is asbout to change.

"Church...at night! What in the world am I doing here?" No way did Jessica want to be there. And she had put up a pretty good argument—until her parents made it pain-fully clear that yes, she would continue to attend the teen class on the life of Jesus. Her church was conducting a 12-week church-wide focus on Jesus. Her parents were in the study in their adult group, and they had told Jessica in no uncertain terms that "you, too, young lady, are going to participate. Besides, it'll be good for all of us."

So there she was, arms folded, glaring and daring anyone to even try to teach her anything. And it was clear she didn't want to talk to anyone either! But just at that moment, a girl sat down next to Jessica, smiled, and said, "Hi, my name's Wendy. What's yours?"

Reflecting on Friendliness

Being friendly and having friends are actually like two sides of the same coin. Part of Jessica's problem was her fear of befriending someone who might once again betray her trust and turn on her. So she chose to be unfriendly, which meant others weren't being friendly to her either.

But Jessica is about to find out that, in spite of her smugness, God wanted three things for her. First of all, He—God Himself!—wanted to personally be her friend. He also wanted to provide friendships for her with others who loved Him, like Wendy. And He wanted Jessica to be friendly and reach out to others—like Jesus did—so others could get a glimpse of what Jesus is like.

You see, God genuinely cares about Jessica—and about you! And He is available at all times. He is a friend who will always be 100 percent faithful, the One you can completely trust for all things.

Do you have a crisis, a concern, or a need? No problem! Just follow these divine instructions and rest in the scripture's promise. And as you read, if it's convenient, pick up a pen or pencil and circle what you are to do—and don't forget to underline the blessed results.

> *Let us then approach the throne of grace with confidence, so that we may receive mercy and find grace to help us in our time of need* (Hebrews 4:16).

Isn't it a relief to know that God is so totally approachable? He's your friend—your very best Number One forever friend. Just think—you can talk things over with Him 24/7, any time, any day. And you can talk to Him about anything. He listens...and He cares. As you walk with Jesus on your journey toward growing more like Him, you'll see Jesus, God in flesh, showing you a character quality you desire—friendliness. And, by the way, when you get a chance, write out some dictionary definitions for the words *approach* and *approachable*.

Jesus Shows You the Way

I'm sure you've been around people who don't seem to be very friendly. Maybe *lots* of people! There's something about them that keeps you from reaching out to them or trying to talk to them. Maybe you need advice, or you have a question you know they can answer, or you want to thank them for something, or you just want to say hi. But something—some invisible wall—keeps you from talking to them. They may be the sweetest, nicest, kindest people on the face of the earth. And what you sense from them may be totally off. But something makes you hesitant to go up to them.

But this was never the case with Jesus when He walked this earth. He—the God of all creation, God in flesh—projected to others that He was warm, available, and welcoming. He was friendly and wanted to build relationships. Notice how He treated a variety of misfits.

The Outcast

In Jesus' day lepers were feared, shunned, and looked down on. They were outcasts from society. In fact, people threw stones at lepers to drive them away. But not Jesus. On one occasion, a leper dared to approach Jesus. What was His response? Jesus "reached out his hand and touched the man" (Mark 1:41)! The result? The leprosy was immediately cured (verse 42).

If you want to be like Jesus, be friendly. Be approachable. Reach out to others, even the unpopular and socially unacceptable "lepers" and outcasts. Learn and live these words spoken from the lips and heart of our wonderful

Jesus. He invited any and all, especially outcasts, to "come to me, all you who are weary and burdened, and I will give you rest" (Matthew 11:28).

A question for your heart: Take a few seconds to go back and notice again what you are to do according to the verses above. Also note or circle what Jesus will do for you. Now, ask yourself a question: Can those who are considered outcasts approach me? Make it a goal to not look down on others. Determine not to ignore those who aren't blessed with position, money, clothes, popularity, intelligence, or health.

Jesus said, "Come to me." What have you learned from Jesus about how to treat people who are left out, unpopular, and ignored? File it away in your heart and make it a part of your life.

The Hopeless

I know you're busy. You have school, homework, chores at home, family and church activities, friends to keep up with, maybe a babysitting or part-time job, and numerouse other activities! So what do you do when someone has a real need? For the answer, it's time to look at Jesus again.

Picture this: Jesus is preaching to a packed house, literally (Mark 2:1-5). Not one additional person could get into the house. As the four friends of a paralyzed man tried to bring their friend to Jesus for help, the crowded house seemed like a hopeless situation. Yet these friends were convinced that Jesus and only Jesus could help their helpless friend. Aggressively and relentlessly, these four guys took the tiles off the roof of the house where Jesus was teaching. Then they lowered their friend's bed down through the hole they had created. Imagine the nerve! And imagine the faith!

At this point Jesus could easily have cried out, "Hey, what's going on? Can't you see I'm busy? Can't you see I'm doing urgent work here, something a lot more important than dealing with your hopeless friend and this interruption? I'm preaching about God here!" But instead, "Jesus saw their faith [and] said to the paralytic, 'Son, your sins are forgiven'" (verse 5). Then Jesus miraculously healed the man. Ministering to this one man was what was important at the moment, even though what He had been doing was important too.

It's the same way when someone—a friend or acquaintance or even your sister—approaches you with a need. Obviously she thinks you can help, and maybe you can. Even if you're busy, this is a good time to ask yourself the question, How would Jesus deal with this girl and her need?

Jesus teaches His followers to be careful not to allow crowds, crowded schedules, and busyness to get in the way of being friendly and available to people who truly need help. The way I try to look at helping the hopeless is like this: I have a lot of friends who are stable, doing okay, and have their lives together. Everything's going great for them…at least for today. They are not facing tough problems or issues. But every so often I meet a woman who is burdened, sad, and has something difficult going on in her life.

What do I do? I've learned to think, *Hey, my friends are doing okay. They can get along without me for a little while so I can talk to this woman, see what's wrong, maybe even pray with her.*

And here's something else I've learned: You (and I) may not always be the one to help someone else or the one who has all the answers. But you can be a part of finding those who can help. Just be a friend who listens, cares, prays, and helps others get the help they need.

A question for your heart: Do you usually rush by, ignore, or avoid people with problems and needs? Ask God to help you make good judgments so you don't neglect sincere cries for help. Also, be willing to help others find the help they need.

The Concerned

You already know how busy you are. And sometimes your busyness can cause others to think twice before approaching you. They're afraid they might be bothering you. After all, you have people to see, places to go, and things to do. So in all your hurrying and focusing on yourself, it's easy to completely miss the concerns of others. Without even knowing it you may be sending a message that says, "Don't you dare bother me now!"

Not so with Jesus. He had every right to refuse to help a high-ranking Roman military officer who approached Him with a concern for one of his servants, who was paralyzed and in agony. Be sure to read about their meeting in Matthew 8:5-13. It went like this:

> Soldier: "Lord…my servant lies at home paralyzed and in terrible suffering."

Jesus: "I will go and heal him."

Soldier: "Lord, I do not deserve to have you come under my roof. But just say the word, and my servant will be healed."

Jesus: "I have not found anyone in Israel with such great faith... Go! It will be done just as you believed it would."

The result: "And his servant was healed at that very hour."

Notice that Jesus wasn't put out or upset by the man's request regarding a mere servant. Even though He had just preached possibly the greatest sermon of all time—the Sermon on the Mount—and was being followed by a massive crowd, amazingly, Jesus paid attention to one man's concern for a lowly servant. In addition, Jesus was willing to actually go to the soldier's house and personally help the man's servant.

A question for your heart: Think about your relationship with Jesus. Do you remember how it began? Can you recall any details? It began because He reached out to you. He approached you. He befriended you. Read the verse below as it appears in the Bible. Then make it personal. Change the word *us* to *me,* and the word *we* to *I.* You can imagine it or write it.

> *God demonstrates his own love for us in this: While we were still sinners, Christ died for us* (Romans 5:8).

God demonstrates his own love for _____
in this: While _____ was still a sinner,
Christ died for _____.

To be more like Jesus, purpose to be more friendly. Pray
to be approachable like He was—and still is—to you today
and every day. Be careful not to put up barriers between
you and those you might be able to help and befriend. Can
you think of several ways you can communicate that you are
available? When you get the chance, list them here or put
them in your prayer journal.

The Unimportant

Who is the most important person who ever lived? You
know the answer, right? It's Jesus Christ. And because He
was such a VIP (Very Important Person), He could also
have been the most separated and protected person who
ever lived, right? But not Jesus. He was just the opposite.
As we're learning, Jesus could be approached by anyone—
from lepers to soldiers, and the sick and the lame.

Maybe you already know the Bible story about Jesus and His love for little children. A scene in Matthew 19 shows us how friendly and approachable He was to both parents and children. The story goes like this:

> *Then little children were brought to Jesus for him to place his hands on them and pray for them. But the disciples rebuked those who brought them. Jesus said, "Let the little children come to me, and do not hinder them, for the kingdom of heaven belongs to such as these." When he had placed his hands on them, he went on from there* (verses 13-15).

Take a minute to think about answers to these questions:

Why were the children brought to Jesus?

What did the disciples do?

What did Jesus do to the disciples?

What did Jesus do to the children?

Obviously the parents of these little ones perceived Jesus was friendly. They felt perfectly comfortable approaching Him with their children. And obviously the disciples thought that Jesus was too important to be bothered by little children. So they tried to send the parents and their children away (verse 13). But they were wrong.

As a Christian, you are important. You are important to Jesus. And you are important to your family and friends. But others are important too. Like those little children (and even your little brothers and sisters!), all are important to Jesus, and they deserve your attention and kindness too.

I work hard on appearing to be friendly and welcoming. Sometimes when I'm at church or speaking at a conference, I sense women hesitating or thinking twice about speaking to me. Some of them even turn away in uncertainty. But my ministry is to women and I truly do want to visit and talk and listen and help. In fact, that's my heart and my joy.

So I've learned to do a few things that help make me appear more available to others. First, I have a personal motto that guides me wherever I go—"Go to give." This is my time with the women, with people. I've come down out of my writing perch to go *out*! And my outing has been prayed over and eagerly anticipated and may be my one and only opportunity to be with a particular group or individual.

Once I get there, I smile—a lot! Then I try to speak to and encourage and touch as many women as I can—a pat on the back here, a squeeze on an arm there, a hug if it's appropriate. I take the initiative and reach out. I don't know if Jesus smiled, but I do know He was a cheerful giver and He was friendly. No one was unimportant to Him, and I want to be like Him!

A question for your heart: What can you do to be more friendly? Here's a list of "Ten Commandments of Friendships" which I put in my book *A Young Woman After God's Own Heart.*[3] As you read, put a checkmark beside the three "commandments" you want to begin to work on.

Speak to people—there is nothing as nice as a cheerful word of greeting.

Smile at people—it takes 72 muscles to frown and only 14 to smile!

Call people by name—the sweetest music to anyone's ear is the sound of their own name.

Be friendly and helpful—if you would have friends, be friendly.

Be cordial—speak and act as if everything you do were a real pleasure.

Be genuinely interested in people—you can like *everyone* if you try.

Be generous with praise—cautious with criticism.

Be considerate of the feelings of others—it will be appreciated.

Be thoughtful of the opinions of others.

Be alert to give service—what counts most in life is what we do for others!

Jesus was friendly, available, and approachable to all kinds of people. He reached out to outsiders, the deaf, the blind, and the lame. He was available to the rich and to the poor and needy. He loved little children and their parents welcomed those who needed a friend and a Savior. And you, my wonderful young friend, get to reflect Him to oh so many who need His love and friendship in a mean and difficult and stressful world.

Reflecting the Heart of Jesus

Being friendly and approachable is a Jesus quality. You may think, *Of course anyone could talk to me or ask something of me.* But you may also be sending a message that says you already have enough friends or you're too busy to be bothered. Or maybe like Jessica, you're sending the message that you don't want any friends. Think again on Jesus' friendliness. Are you sure you are friendly and approachable? To your family at home? To the people at school, at church, or next door? Is your heart tuned in to those who are outcasts, hopeless, concerned and needy, seemingly unimportant—the outsiders?

Jesus meant it when He said, "Come to me, all you who are weary and burdened, and I will give you rest" (Matthew 11:28). Ask God to look into your heart. Pray for an approachable spirit that will reflect the heart of Jesus, the One who never refused the cries of anyone who needed a friend and some help...including you.

A Prayer to Pray

Lord Jesus, I can't believe that You are my friend! Thank You that You are always available to me when I have a problem. You are always right here with me when I'm alone or lonely. I know how good it feels to have a friend like You, and I want to reflect Your heart and be a Jesus kind of friend to others. Help me be available to others who need Your help through me. Give me open eyes and an open heart. And thanks again for being my best friend! Amen.

Want to Know More About...
Being Friendly?

Proverbs 17:17—Write out this verse:

What are two things that mark a true friend?

—

—

What do these three verses add to the marks of a true friend?

Proverbs 18:24—

Philippians 2:4—

1 Thessalonians 5:11—

Romans 15:7—Write out the command in this verse and the standard for it.

What do these verses say about those who are not to be your friends?

Proverbs 13:20—

Proverbs 22:24—

Proverbs 23:20—

Which of these verses were your favorites or the most challenging, and why?

5

★ ★ ★ ★

Gracious

Say, "Please"

Jessica just loved where she lived. Growing up in a state where the sun shines most of the year was perfect for sunbathing, water skiing, and swimming in her friend Mary's pool. And like the great weather, another element of Southern living and hospitality was being groomed by her mom in the fine art of being socially gracious…which was not something Jessica liked at all!

Like a family tradition that's handed down from generation to generation, Jessica and her friends were taught by their moms to be gracious and to practice good etiquette, especially in public. Their graciousness was a "learned behavior" and was what was expected of children who were "well bred," who were brought up "right." Because this graciousness was external, or outside behavior only, it could be easily turned on and off just like a light switch. Graciousness became a character quality that Jessica could play whenever it was required or expected...or got her something she wanted. Even Jessica knew she could be a perfect picture of graciousness when she wanted something, but she could just as easily turn into a mean girl and an ugly brat. All she had to do was flip the "graciousness switch" off.

As Jessica wandered into this week's Bible study meeting, she was thinking to herself, *Maybe, just maybe that's why I don't have very many friends.* And you know what? Maybe, just maybe that was true. Nobody wanted to cross Jessica's path when her graciousness switch was off, so they avoided her like the plague. But somehow Wendy, her friend from church, tolerated her moods. And Wendy always showed a genuinely gracious spirit toward Jessica and everyone else. This was hard for Jessica to understand because she was constantly turning her good behavior switch on and off.

But what Wendy exhibited—and Jessica couldn't understand—was the real kindness that the Bible talks about. Wendy always showed a gracious attitude that was truly from the heart, that was authentic. It wasn't something she turned on and off, but something that was prominently embedded in the core of her being. It was something that could only come from Jesus.

Well, hang on, for Jessica is about to see for herself the ultimate example of graciousness in this week's lesson on the life of Jesus.

Jesus Shows You the Way

Jesus. Just say His name and the word *grace* snaps into my mind, and maybe in yours too. Jesus was gracious, giving, and generous. He extended the marvelous grace of His salvation to sinners like you and me. As we look now at this marvelous virtue on our walk through Jesus' life and His character qualities, it's no surprise by now that we find this character trait fully and perfectly lived out by our Lord. Thank goodness, because that means we have someone we can look to and copy.

In today's culture, a gracious person is usually someone who shows respect, honor, and kindness to others. She always seems to say the right thing (such as "Please" and "Thank you"), do the right thing, and act in the right way. In Bible times a gracious person was usually someone in a high position who showed favor and mercy to another person in a lesser position with little or no power, someone less important. For instance, in the Old Testament you can read about...

> Potiphar, who dealt graciously with his slave, Joseph (Genesis 39:4);
>
> the needy Ruth, who found favor in the eyes of Boaz (Ruth 2:10);
>
> the young Jewish girl Esther, who was treated graciously by King Ahasuerus (Esther 2:17; 5:2);
>
> and God, who was gracious toward mankind, who describes Himself as "the LORD, the compassionate and gracious God" (Exodus 34:6).

And in the New Testament, God's grace is a demonstration of His love. Aren't you glad God deals with His people through grace and not on the basis of what we deserve, or on our worth, or our behavior? God is good and generous, and so is His grace. The greatest example of God's grace is seen and experienced in all that God has done for you and me through Christ.[4]

As we look at Jesus, we can't miss the beauty of the Son of God. He was the very image of the Father, *full* of grace! There was no on-off switch for His graciousness. No, He exhibited gracious behavior at all times during His days on earth. As you make your way through the following scenes from His life, be on the lookout for His courteous way with people. You'll see a few people you've met up with before in this book, but in this chapter we are focusing on the grace of our Lord to people like you and me.

Words That Hurt, Words That Heal

Jesus was a teacher, and a teacher must teach. The Bible tells us that on one occasion, "on the Sabbath day he went into the synagogue, as was his custom" (Luke 4:16). After reading from the Scriptures Jesus sat down to explain what they meant. What was the response of those who heard Him that day? "All spoke well of him and were amazed at the gracious words that came from his lips" (verse 22).

Jesus' ministry was characterized by grace. His words were both kind and wise. He didn't practice flattery or exaggerate. He didn't beat people up with His language. And His words weren't just nice and sweet. He wasn't trying to woo or wow the people with His speech. No, instead He spoke truth with authority because He spoke words from God. What was important was that the people understood what He was saying because His words were the words of life, words that would set them free from their sins.

I'm sure you've been around people who do beat you up with their words and tone of voice. You've been on the receiving end of words that tear you down. And you know what it's like to hear words that lift you up. So I'm sure you want to make sure you are an encourager to others. You want to be like Jesus and help others and make their life easier. Is your pen ready? Here are a couple verses that show you the difference. Mark them up, making sure you notice the opposites, or mark them later if this isn't a good time.

> *Do not let any unwholesome talk come out of your mouths, but only what is helpful for building others up according to their needs* (Ephesians 4:29).

What is the command here?

How is gracious speech described?

What is the goal and result of gracious speech?

Reckless words pierce like a sword, but the tongue of the wise brings healing (Proverbs 12:18).

Words have great power! What negative use of words do you see in this verse?

And what positive use of words do you see?

What first step will you take to stop using words that hurt and start using words that heal? Be specific.

A question for your heart: As a Christian daughter, sister, friend, and student, you are a young woman who can—and should—represent Jesus to others. The source of your speech is your very own heart. So far, what kind of words and speech has your heart produced? How do you talk to your parents and your brothers and sisters? When you walk by God's Spirit, then His love, patience, goodness, kindness, gentleness, and self-control are present. These are the fruit of His Spirit (Galatians 5:22-23). When you are walking with Jesus, you reflect Him. Then your choice of words will display these God-like qualities.

Grace Under Fire

Meet poor Martha—you'll run into her several times in this book. When you read Luke 10:38-42, you'll see that Martha definitely lost control. In this brief sketch, she graciously opened her home to Jesus and His 12 disciples. Serving and hosting this large group was a lot of work! In the beginning, her sister, Mary, helped her. But when Jesus began teaching, Mary planted herself at His feet and was all ears.

Well, Martha lost her cool...and her manners. She burst into the room, interrupted the Teacher, slandered Mary, and lit into the Lord, accusing Him of not caring.

Wow! Aren't you embarrassed for Martha? But note Jesus' tender grace as He responded to her impatience and frustration, her bad attitude and condemning speech.

> *Martha, Martha...you are worried and upset about many things, but only one thing is*

needed. Mary has chosen what is better, and it will not be taken away from her (Luke 10:41-42).

Jesus could have dealt harshly with Martha. She had dealt harshly with Him and with Mary. She had opened fire, so to speak, and let Him have it! Yes, she certainly deserved to be rebuked. But that wasn't Jesus' style. He acted with grace under fire. First He graciously spoke her name twice, which scholars tell us is a sign of tender love and endearment. Then He acknowledged her concerns about doing so much work in preparing the house and meal so He and the disciples would feel welcomed and cared for. But He also let her know she had missed the point of her giving and service. Jesus wanted to gently show her the real priority, the "good part" that she was missing out on—knowing, hearing, and worshiping Him.

A question for your heart: How patient are you when someone misses the point of your communication, or misses out on noticing your needs, or misses the big picture? How gracious are you with these people? You can get mad and upset. You can rant and rave. You can let others have it with your words. And you can rationalize your actions all you want. But the situations and pressures you face every day are to be handled in a Christlike manner—with graciousness. Be patient and kind to those who aren't where you are, or haven't quite grasped the bigger picture. Be gracious and follow Jesus' example and Paul's exhortation to "slander no one, to be peaceable and considerate, and to show true humility toward all" (Titus 3:2).

How Can I Help?

Compassion and mercy are similar to graciousness. A gracious person is usually a compassionate person, and a compassionate person is usually gracious. These qualities are like two sides of the same coin. Jesus showed these two attitudes together as He passed through Jericho on His way to Jerusalem. As He was leaving Jericho, two blind beggars called out to Him. Here's what happened:

> *Then the multitude warned [the two blind beggars] that they should be quiet; but they cried out all the more, saying, "Have mercy on us, O Lord, Son of David!" So Jesus stood still and called them, and said, "What do you want Me to do for you?" They said to Him, "Lord, that our eyes may be opened." So Jesus had compassion and touched their eyes. And immediately their eyes received sight, and they followed Him* (Matthew 20:31-34 NKJV).

How did the crowd treat the blind men?

What did the blind men ask of Jesus before asking to be healed?

What key word describes the difference between the crowd's attitude toward these two men and Jesus' attitude?

Jesus healed a lot of people during His three years of ministry. Those who were blind and sick never stopped coming to Him. And the amazing thing is that there is no record of His refusing any of them who approached Him for help. But note Jesus' graciousness in this example. These needy beggars were told by everyone to be quiet and stop calling out to Jesus as He went by. But Jesus heard them, stopped, asked them what they wanted from Him, and then did as they asked. Unlike the people, He treated them graciously and with respect. They were human beings, and they had needs and were suffering. Filled with mercy and compassion, He graciously extended the grace of God to them by healing them and restoring their sight.

A question for your heart: The grace we witness in the Bible is defined as God's unmerited favor offered to those who don't deserve it. Jesus asked these men, "What do you want Me to do for you?" Now consider yourself: Are you a gracious person? Do you have—and show—this kind of concern for others? If so, you are reflecting Jesus. You are radiating the great and gracious heart of Jesus. If you need a grace prod, put this at the top of your daily prayer list: "God, help me remember to be gracious today." Then when you are out and about, ask others, "What can

I do to help you today?" Or ask your heart whenever you run into others, "What can I do to bless this person I'm with right now?" Looking at others through eyes of love will result in gracious words and works.

Don't Give Up on Your Friends

Peter was seen as the leader of the disciples. He is listed first each time the disciples are named in Scripture. He was also the spokesman for the group. And Jesus even referred to Peter as a "rock" (Matthew 16:18). It's no wonder Jesus was counting on Peter to lead the other disciples after He went up into heaven.

The night before Jesus was betrayed, He knew exactly what was going to happen when He and the 12 disciples left the upper room, where they ate the Last Supper. He knew Peter would deny Him. In fact, He even told Peter what was going to happen. He looked at Peter and graciously said, "Simon, Simon! Indeed, Satan has asked for you, that he may sift you as wheat. But I have prayed for you, that your faith should not fail; and when you have returned to Me, strengthen your brethren" (Luke 22:31 NKJV).

Jesus never gave up on Peter, no matter what he did or how he acted. The all-knowing Jesus knew everything about Peter's shortcomings. But, instead of washing His hands and walking away from Peter, Jesus still believed the best for Peter and prayed that he would bounce back from his failure.

A question for your heart: It's always good to have family and friends you can depend on. They're there when you need them, and you can count on them to come through for you. (And, of course, I hope this is true of you too as their friend.) But at times people fail. That brings up this question: How do you act—or react—when someone lets you down? Do you follow the natural responses of blowing up, or letting your friend have it, or putting her down, or walking away from the friendship? Follow Jesus' example instead. Try to show some grace. Try to understand what might have happened that caused this person to let you down. Like Jesus, who saw the good in Peter, look beyond the failure and remember the good.

The Proverbs 31 Woman Shows You the Way

Throughout your life as a woman—young or old, single or married—you'll love the Proverbs 31 woman. She is God's ideal woman, and you can read about her in Proverbs 31:10-31. She was indeed a gracious and godly woman. God launches His description of her many sterling character qualities with a question...and an answer: "Who can find a virtuous woman? For her price is far above rubies" (Proverbs 31:10 KJV). God's excellent woman has graciousness stamped on every part of her nature.

Let's take a little mini-walk through her incredible qualities. Use your pen to circle, underline, or doodle in the margins—whatever it takes to get God's message to your heart. And don't forget to write out any "notes to self" as God speaks to your heart.

What do people see when this gracious woman walks into a room? What defines her conduct? "She is clothed with strength and dignity" (verse 25).

What is her attitude toward others, especially the less fortunate? "She opens her arms to the poor and extends her hands to the needy" (verse 20).

What is the manner of her speech? "She speaks with wisdom, and faithful instruction is on her tongue" (verse 26).

What is the key to her character? "Charm is deceptive, and beauty is fleeting; but a woman who fears the LORD is to be praised" (verse 30).

Reflecting the Heart of Jesus

Think about this: Jesus was perfectly gracious. Because of His love, He was warm, courteous, and kind. He didn't merely turn on graciousness when needed and then turn around and turn it off. No, Jesus was gracious in nature. That means He was gracious all the time. It was part of His nature.

And that's how you can reflect the gracious heart of Jesus. You reflect Him when your heart overflows with His love, when your lips overflow with kind and encouraging words. When you extend this gracious spirit of the Lord, people will feel welcome and cared for when they're in your presence. And best of all, as you act and speak with the grace of God, people will be drawn to Jesus.

⌁ A Prayer to Pray ⌁

Gracious Lord, what can I say but thank You for the wonderful grace You show toward me? I know that Your mercy and compassion are completely unde-served. I can't believe how much You love me in spite of myself and how I act sometimes. Please help me love You even more. And please help me to extend Your graciousness to others. Amen.

Want to Know More About...
Being Gracious?

As you read these verses in your Bible, note the kinds of speech you should have—and not have—and why.

Psalm 19:14—

Proverbs 12:25—

Proverbs 25:11—

Ephesians 4:25—

Ephesians 4:29—

Ephesians 4:31—

Colossians 4:6—

James 1:19-20—

Which of these verses were your favorites or the most challenging, and why?

6

★ ★ ★ ★

Prayerful
God's Heavenly Hotline

 It has now been more than a month since Jessica's youth group began a Bible study on the life of Jesus. To Jessica's praise, she has really tried to take to heart what she's been learning. And it certainly hasn't been easy! Like the saying tells us, Old habits die hard. They are hard to break, and Jessica had her share of well-entrenched bad habits that she had been nurturing for about 16 years.

But, to her amazement, Jessica was showing definite signs of spiritual growth. She was beginning to give off a much clearer reflection of Jesus. First her parents noticed a difference in her actions and attitudes toward them. That made things much nicer at home! And even Jessica's brother, Jason, and her sister, Jenny, had complimented and remarked on how cool their sister was becoming. (To them her transformation was nothing short of a miracle!)

From what Jessica had learned some weeks ago, she

had especially been trying to be faithful in all areas of her life. Again, it hadn't been easy. Her progress was usually something like three steps forward and two steps back. But through it all Jessica was progressing, and she knew it. And she liked the new Jessica.

As Jessica eagerly entered the youth center looking for her new real friend, Wendy, she had no idea that the two of them together were about to learn a powerful lesson from the life of Jesus—a lesson about being prayerful.

Jesus Shows You the Way

I think you would definitely agree with me when I say that prayer is difficult. Yes, prayer is a blessing and a rich spiritual experience. But maybe because we're so busy, or we lack faith in the power of prayer, or whatever the cause might be, we (or at least I) don't pray as often or as fervently as we should. And once again, as always and in all things, as we look at this virtue of prayerfulness, Jesus is the perfect model. When we learned about Jesus' faithfulness in an earlier chapter, we saw that He lived in a spirit of prayer. No matter where He was or what was happening around Him or to Him, He prayed. Prayer was Jesus' life, His habit. He talked everything over with His Father. Nothing was too small to merit His prayers.

If you're not happy with your prayer life (and who isn't?), then learning more about Jesus' habit of prayer can be very inspiring. He shows you the way to a more faithful and consistent prayer life.

What Is the Right Thing to Do?

When we read through the Gospels, we see many portraits of Jesus at prayer. You can't miss the fact that Jesus made it His habit to pray before important events and about important decisions in His life. For instance...

Jesus prayed as He began His ministry—Jesus' baptism was a significant milestone in His life and ministry. It announced the beginning of His public ministry. How did Jesus approach this important occasion? "When all the people were being baptized, Jesus was baptized too. And as he was praying, heaven was opened and the Holy Spirit descended on him in bodily form like a dove" (Luke 3:21-22).

This baptism was the first decision Jesus made when He began His ministry. And immediately, as a part of this ceremony, we find Him offering up His first recorded instance of prayer.

Jesus prayed as He chose His disciples—Jesus had many followers, but He desired to choose 12 as leaders, as apostles, as "sent ones." These men would be given the task of delivering His message to the world. Their selection would mark the beginning of the focused training of a few people who would take the gospel to the ends of the earth. This was definitely a historic occasion. How in the world would Jesus choose just 12 people from all those who followed Him? I hope your pencil is handy as you read on!

> *One of those days Jesus went out to a mountain-side to pray, and spent the night praying to God. When morning came, he called his disciples to*

him and chose twelve of them, whom he also designated apostles (Luke 6:12-13).

What did Jesus do in preparation for making His decision (verse 12)?

Where did this occur?

How long did Jesus pray before selecting the 12 disciples?

A question for your heart: What decision are you facing today? Are you wondering what is the right thing to do? Your decision may or may not seem as significant as the choosing of 12 men to carry on a ministry. But whatever it is, it merits—and requires—your prayers. Most of the decisions you make may not seem very important. But every choice you make can have a great impact on your future. Therefore it's wise to always seek God's will through prayer so that every choice you make has a better chance of being the right choice.

Jesus prayed before going to the cross—In this scenario, Jesus' time on earth was coming to a close. His training of the disciples was almost over. He knew His death on the cross was ahead of Him, and He knew what that meant for all mankind. So He moved with His disciples to the Garden of Gethsemane. The crucifixion would be extremely painful and difficult, and His soul was in agony. How did He handle this difficult decision according to Matthew 26:39?

> *Going a little farther, he fell with his face to the ground and prayed, "My Father, if it is possible, may this cup be taken from me. Yet not as I will, but as you will."*

What was His request?

The Lord's anguish had nothing to do with fear over the physical torture He would face at the cross or even His death. No, He was sorrowful because judgment for all sin would soon fall on His shoulders. How did Jesus handle this horrendous situation? He prayed.

> *He went away a second time and prayed, "My Father, if it is not possible for this cup to be taken away unless I drink it, may your will be done"* (verse 42).

As Jesus prayed this second time, how did His prayer change?

You and I will never know or experience anything like Jesus did as He prepared for, faced, and endured death on a cross. But we do suffer—physical pain, emotional pain, difficult circumstances, needs in our life, challenging relationships, and more. To prepare for, face, and endure your suffering, you know what you need to do, right? Do what Jesus did and pray!

Jesus shows you and all Christians the importance of praying before you make a decision so that you can gain God's direction. Jesus' habit of prayer shows you how to tap into God's power and wisdom. His desire was to follow the Father's will completely, and prayer was a vital part of His decision making. And you should view prayer in the same way.

A question for your heart: As you think about your life and the days ahead, what important event is about to occur? What guidance do you need for your future? Are you deciding about whether to go to college, or which college? Whether to allow a friendship or relationship to continue with that certain boy, especially if your parents don't approve? Do you need to get a job, or choose between different jobs? Follow Jesus' example and pray. God has given you the resource of prayer. Hear His words now:

Ask and it will be given to you; seek and you will find; knock and the door will be opened to you. For everyone who asks receives; he who seeks finds; and to him who knocks, the door will be opened (Matthew 7:7-8).

What does Jesus want you to do when you face an issue or experience a need?

Let us then approach the throne of grace with confidence, so that we may receive mercy and find grace to help us in our time of need (Hebrews 4:16).

According to this verse, what else does the Bible teach about coming to Jesus with your needs?

Praying for Others

Intercession for others—that is, mediating and praying for them to the Father—marked the prayers of Jesus during His time on earth.

For instance (and you may be familiar with this scene), on the night before His death, Jesus told His disciple Peter that the devil had asked permission to test Peter with a severe trial. Jesus said,

> *Simon, Simon, Satan has asked to sift you as wheat. But I have prayed for you, Simon, that your faith may not fail. And when you have turned back, strengthen your brothers* (Luke 22:31-32).

After Jesus gave His warning, what comfort did He give to Peter in verse 32?

Later on that same dreadful night, just hours before His death, Jesus prayed His great "intercessory prayer" in John 17. Here's an outline of the general content of His famous prayer for others, including you and me.

- First our Lord prayed for Himself, that He would glorify the Father (verses 1-5).

- Next Jesus prayed in intercession for His disciples (verses 6-19). He prayed that the Father would "protect them from the evil one" and "sanctify them by the truth" of God's Word.

- Then Jesus looked toward the future and prayed for all who would become believers, including you and me. He prayed for our unity, for the indwelling of the Spirit, and that one day all believers would be with Him in heaven (verses 20-26).

The book of Hebrews contains an amazing statement about the ministry Jesus is carrying on right now:

> *He is able to save completely those who come to God through him, because he always lives to intercede for them* (Hebrews 7:25).

What do you learn here about Jesus' present ministry of intercession?

Are you touched? You should be! Just think: The God of the universe is interceding on your behalf right now. What are your current struggles or temptations? List a few of them here. Then pray and give thanks that Jesus is interceding for you.

As we look at Jesus' ministry of praying for others, we can only conclude that if it was important for Him to do this, it should be important for us as well. We are instructed to...

> *pray for each other so that you may be healed. The prayer of a righteous man is powerful and effective* (James 5:16).

According to this verse, what is your responsibility to others not only when they are sick, but for any and all reasons?

Jesus' prayers for others serve as a powerful reminder that you too should pray for others. Again, I know you are busy. But, like Peter and the disciples, you are in a fierce spiritual battle, and so are those you know. So like Jesus, pray for yourself and your trials and decisions. And then pray for others—your family, your friends, your teachers, and so on. You can even pray for Christians around the world!

A question for your heart: How does knowing that Jesus is interceding for you give you confidence as you live your life for Him? You can use the space below to answer. And while you're praying, resolve to follow Jesus' example and pray for others. Think of all the great things you can pray for—their walk with God, protection from the evil one, their holiness, unity among the leaders and kids in your youth group, wisdom for your pastor. You'll love being linked with the Lord in His work in the lives of those you pray for.

Don't Be a Show-off

When Jesus delivered His great Sermon on the Mount, He pointed out a practice among some of the people, especially the religious leaders, who wanted to be seen as "holy." These phonies used public prayer as a way to show off and call attention to themselves. Jesus called them "hypocrites" (Matthew 6:5). Then He gave instructions for sincere prayer:

> *When you pray, go into your room, close the door and pray to your Father, who is unseen. Then your Father, who sees what is done in secret, will reward you* (verse 6).

In contrast to the hypocrites, how and where are you to pray?

What will the result be?

Your prayers are for private communion with God. He and He alone is the audience. He and He alone is the One you are addressing. That doesn't mean public prayer isn't appropriate. But it does mean that before you pray in public, you should search your heart for your reasons and motives for doing so. Public prayer is not a competition. We're not to use it as a chance to show off. No, prayer is between you and God. It is communion with God that matters, not impressing other people.

Reflecting the Heart of Jesus

For Jesus, prayer was like breathing. It's as if He couldn't live without it. His every breath taken in was exhaled as a prayer.

By now you know a lot about the content of Jesus' prayers. His foremost desire was to fulfill the Father's will. In His last prayer to the Father before His death on the cross, He said, "I have brought you glory on earth by completing the work you gave me to do" (John 17:4). Jesus used prayer as a major tool for accomplishing the goal of fulfilling God's will.

The blessings of prayer await you. The blessings of communing with God. The blessings of dealing with sin and growing more and more into the image of Jesus. The blessings of talking things over with God before you make your decisions...and before you make too many mistakes! And the blessings of loving and caring for others enough to ask God to help them and work in their lives. Best of all, building the habit of prayer into your daily routine builds Christlike character into your life.

All of this—and more!—is accomplished through prayer. As the great Protestant reformer Martin Luther wrote, "The less I pray, the harder it gets; the more I pray, the better it goes." So, in the words of another saint, "The main lesson about prayer is just this: Do it! Do it! Do it! You want to be taught to pray? [The] answer is: pray."[5] That's a sure way to reflect the great heart of Jesus.

⁓ A Prayer to Pray ⁓

Jesus, I know I need to get serious about praying about my problems and dreams. Thank You for showing me how important it is to seek Your direction before I make a decision. I look forward to the many blessings of being a woman of prayer. Help me to become a young woman after Your heart who prays faithfully...just like You did. Amen.

Want to Know More About... Praying?

When the disciples asked Jesus, "Lord, teach us to pray" (Luke 11:1), He gave them—and you—a model prayer. Look at this prayer, usually referred to as the Lord's Prayer, in your Bible in Matthew 6:9-13. Then answer the questions that guide you through an outline of the contents of this great prayer.

Prayer is offered as an act of worship. How is God to be addressed (verse 9)?

Prayer is offered with reverence. How is God's name to be spoken (verse 9)?

Prayer is offered with anticipation. What event did God promise to establish in the future (verse 10)?

Prayer is offered selflessly. What should be the desire of your heart (verse 10)?

Prayer is offered for personal needs. What should be the limit of your request (verse 11)?

Prayer is offered for spiritual needs. When asking for forgiveness, what is assumed toward others (verse 12)?

Prayer is offered for spiritual protection. What two requests are made (verse 12)?

—

—

A word of encouragement: The best way for you to learn how to pray is to follow Jesus' model. Do what He said and pray as He prayed. The Lord prayed at all times for all things, and so can you. Jesus prayed faithfully and earnestly, and so can you. And He prayed for the good of God's people, and so can you. So start praying. You're in for a thrill!

7

★ ★ ★ ★

Pure

What Is Your Standard?

"When I say the word *purity,* what comes to your mind?"

Oh boy, here it comes, Jessica thought to herself as she shifted uneasily in her chair. The boys and girls had split up for the first portion of this week's class on the life of Jesus. The youth leader's wife, Rebecca, took the girls to the far side of the youth hall for "The Talk." But to Jessica's surprise, Rebecca took the talk in a different direction than she had expected.

"Obviously as women," Rebecca explained, "when someone says the word *purity,* we tend to think of sexual purity. But purity has broader meanings. *Purity* basically means that nothing is added or taken away from our minds or our spirits that is not consistent with the character of God."

Rebecca's wisdom and presentation was starting to draw Jessica into her talk, and in a loving and absorbing way she continued to talk about purity.

"Purity," she said, "has become a strange and foreign concept in our society today. Nothing is the real thing. That's because something has been added or taken away from just about everything we know and use today. But there is one thing, or should I say 'one Person,' from whom nothing had been added to or taken away from for all eternity. God is the only pure being in the whole universe."

The Holiness and Purity of God

To begin, God is totally separate from all His creation. He is unique and holy. This uniqueness is affirmed in Exodus 15:11 with two questions. What is the obvious answer to each question?

Question #1—"Who among the gods is like you, O LORD?"

Answer:

Question #2—"Who is like you—majestic in holiness, awesome in glory, working wonders?"

Answer:

Because God is holy, He is absolutely pure and good. Therefore He is untouchable and unstained by the evil in

admitted, "We are punished justly, for we are getting what our deeds deserve. But this man has done nothing wrong." Then he said, "Jesus, remember me when you come into your kingdom." Jesus answered, "I tell you the truth, today you will be with me in paradise" (Luke 23:41-43). The thief's response? He acknowledged his sinfulness.

The thief admitted that his death sentence was deserved, and he testified of Jesus' innocence. He recognized Jesus' righteousness and holiness and responded in faith.

The soldiers at the cross—If I were writing a biographical novel, I might describe the scene of the crucifixion something like this:

> The day started out with "business as usual" for the centurion soldier and his men as they went to work. Unfortunately their work included herding condemned prisoners to a place where they were to be executed by the most painful of all deaths—crucifixion. Their job was not to judge, only to carry out the judgment of others. On this day they escorted three men to be executed. But something unusual was about to happened on this particular day.
>
> One of the prisoners was different than any other man they had ever marched to their death. His name was Jesus and His only crime was that of being King of the Jews. After all of the trials, examinations, and interrogations, this was Jesus' only crime. His purity as the perfect sacrifice was again affirmed.
>
> The soldiers watched as events began to

unfold: darkness fell, tombs were opened around them and the dead came out, and even in death this Jesus seemed to be different. These rough and brutal soldiers could only come to one conclusion. "They were terrified, and exclaimed, 'Surely he was the Son of God!'" (Matthew 27:54).

While the religious leaders were celebrating Jesus' death, these heathen men recognized His innocence. They observed Jesus' unusual responses to His suffering and dying. Their response? They were the first to proclaim Jesus as the Son of God after His death. Unfortunately, even though the soldiers recognized Jesus as the Son of God, we see no evidence that they responded in faith.

A question for your heart: You have just read four different responses to Jesus. What's yours? Think about it, and be sure to thank Him and praise Him with every breath and respond in obedience by seeking to live a pure life.

Understanding More About Purity

Purity is high on God's list for women—It's very clear in the Bible that God wants His women—young, old, and all ages—to be pure. In Titus 2:3-5 God tells the older women in the church to teach and serve as role models to the younger women. It's amazing that there are only six topics listed for them to teach to those who are younger. And guess what? Purity is one of them: "Older women likewise are to be reverent...teaching what is good, so that they may encourage the young women to...[be] pure" (NASB). This most definitely places your purity—both spiritual and physical—high on God's list! Can you think of some steps you are taking or could be taking to keep purity high on your list of things "to do and to be"? You can write them here.

A question for your heart: Why do you think purity should be a character quality in young women who want to follow Jesus?

More specifically, why do you think purity should be a character quality in you?

Purity doesn't just happen—Because of our sin nature, purity doesn't come naturally. In fact, the opposite is what comes naturally! So you must make an effort to avoid people, places, and practices that might tempt you toward wrong thoughts and deeds. Here's a verse that gives you three steps you can take in order to insure purity:

*Flee the evil desires of youth, and pursue righ-
teousness, faith, love and peace, along with
those who call on the Lord out of a pure heart*
(2 Timothy 2:22).

Step #1: What are you to avoid?

Step #2: What are you to pursue instead?

—   —

—   —

Step #3: Who are you to associate with?

A question for your heart: Take a good look at your
best friends. Are they helping to contribute to your purity?
Are they "those who call on the Lord out of a pure heart"?
Always remember what God says: "Do not be misled: 'Bad
company corrupts good character'" (1 Corinthians 15:33),

and "You must not associate with anyone who calls himself a brother [a Christian] but is sexually immoral" (1 Corinthians 5:11).

Purity comes from God's Word—God's Word is good for everything—including purity. In fact, God's Word itself is pure. Psalm 19:8 says, "The commandment of the LORD is pure" (NKJV), and Psalm 119:140 says, "Your word is very pure" (NKJV). Also, 1 Peter 2:2 tells believers to "desire the pure milk of the word" (NKJV). A daily dose of the Bible will have a powerful purifying effect on your heart and mind.

Reading the Word will lead you to a purer life, and you'll be blessed even more as you take time to memorize God's Word. Psalm 119:9,11 gives this advice to young adults: "How can a young man keep his way pure? By living according to your word...I have hidden your word in my heart that I might not sin against you."

A question for your heart: God Himself is telling you that there is something special and unique about His Word, the Bible. In fact, it's crucial to your purity. It has the ability to not only give you guidance in your relationships with young men, but also to keep you from sexual sin and from making devastating decisions that can negatively affect you for life. Here's a saying that is so true: "Either the Bible will keep you from sin, or sin will keep you from the Bible."

How can you increase the amount of time you spend each day reading your Bible? To help you establish the habit of reading God's Word, I have included a "Quiet Times Calendar" for you in the back of this book. The idea is for you to read something—anything!—in your Bible each day and, as you do so, you can mark the calendar with an X (or fill it in with a color pencil or pen) to show your progress. As you are faithful in this one small but vital practice, you will contribute to safeguarding your purity

Purity comes from confession—What is another step you can and must take on the road to purity? Read on:

> *If we confess our sins, he is faithful and just and will forgive us our sins and purify us from all unrighteousness* (1 John 1:9).

When you confess your sins, you are acknowledging your disobedience and thanking God that His Son Jesus has dealt with your sins on the cross. To confess your sin means to agree with God about the times you fail to live according to His standard of purity. Jesus, the one who died for your sins, is ready to forgive you!

Reflecting the Heart of Jesus

God's goal for you is purity and holiness. And purity includes your mind and thoughts as well as your conduct. It requires that you carefully watch over what you see, read, and hear, as well as the friends you spend time with.

When it comes to purity, you want to...

> ...guard your physical purity. This will guide how you behave.

> ...guard your mental purity. This will dictate what you think.

> ...guard your spiritual purity. This will determine the depth of your devotion and worship.

The prayer of your heart and the goal of your life should be to live pure and holy. And your model is Jesus. He alone is the standard by which you are to measure your conduct. He alone is the perfect model to copy. Like all the areas of your life, God expects you to manage your purity. He has entrusted you with this most precious possession. Guard it well!

∽ *My Prayer for Purity* ∼

Lord…
I give You all the desires of my heart—
    may You bring them into line with
    Your perfect will.
I give You my mind—
    may it be filled with thoughts that could be
    brought into Your holy presence.
I give You my mouth—
    may I speak only that which honors You,
    encourages others, and reveals a pure heart.
I give You my body—
    may I keep my body pure so that it is
    a holy and honorable vessel, fit for Your use.
I give You my friendships with men—
    may I set my heart on purity.
    May You have authority over all my passions.
I give myself afresh to You.
    Take my life and let it be
    ever, always, pure for Thee.[6]

Want to Know More About...
Purity?

A young woman who reflects the heart of Jesus dresses in a way that reflects His purity. What do these verses say about what you are to wear and not wear?

Proverbs 31:25—

1 Timothy 2:9-10—

1 Peter 3:2-4—

According to Romans 13:14, what are you to clothe yourself with, and what is to be your goal?

What do these verses say about your purity and what is commanded?

Philippians 4:8—

James 1:27—

1 Thessalonians 4:3—

1 John 3:3—

Which of these verses were your favorites or the most challenging, and why?

8

★ ★ ★ ★

Responsible

You Can Count on Me

"Oh, no!" Jessica gasped. She was looking at herself in the mirror as she quickly tried to pull herself together in the girls' bathroom at school before dashing out into the hall to race the last few feet to her first class for the day. "Phew," she exhaled as she just barely made it through the classroom door before the bell rang. She definitely couldn't afford to be late to class again.

Earlier that morning, Jessica's bad day began when she had punched her snooze button one too many times. No wonder she was behind on everything. When she finally did roll out of bed, she had only enough time to literally throw on some clothes, rush out the door with a Pop-Tart in hand, and barely catch the school bus as it was pulling away from the pickup point.

Sleeping in was only the tip of Jessica's iceberg of irresponsibility. You see, Jessica was queen of the "undisciplineds."

She had a reputation for being late, not keeping her word, and not taking care of her roles and responsibilities. She gave a new meaning to the word *slacker* because she was always doing as little as possible to get by.

But today, for some reason, something was definitely different. as Jessica had realized it while she was looking in the girls' bathroom mirror. Then it hit her like a ton of bricks. *Maybe, just maybe it's those lessons on the life of Jesus! I hate to admit it, but I'm enjoying learning more about Jesus. Talk about someone who had His act together! I can hardly believe it, but I'm actually looking forward to the next study tonight.*

A Personal Note

As parents of two girls, Jim and I have logged thousands (which sometimes felt like millions!) of hours training, hoping, and praying for our daughters to be responsible. We took parenting classes, read books, and met with other parents as we tried to learn how to instill this trait of all traits into our two daughters. We even developed a system of assigning our girls a new responsibility, carefully teaching them how to take care of that task, and then rewarding them for being responsible in that area. We called it "learn one, earn one." This means once they knew what they were supposed to do and learned how to do it and proved to be responsible for it, they earned a privilege or a reward.

I'll never forget the day when our older daughter, Katherine, got her driver's license. She begged and pleaded with us for days, maybe even weeks, to let her drive herself and her sister, Courtney, to high school. No way did she want us taking her. And no way did she want to stay in a car pool. Finally Jim agreed.

Now, one reason we hesitated about letting Katherine use the car was because it left me stranded at home without any way of doing my shopping. So after Katherine agreed that she would run my errands for me after she finished school, I got on board with the plan.

Day 1 finally arrived. I prayed with the girls, waved good-bye to them, walked back into the house, and fell on my knees and prayed until Katherine called me from school. She had made it—hooray! At 3:00 I hit the floor to pray again as she was leaving school and heading for the grocery store. She had my list, enough cash for the purchase, and I had guessed she and Courtney would arrive home about 3:45. Was I ever surprised when the front door opened at 3:15 and in they walked.

I did what every mom tries to remember to do—I asked if everything was okay, were there any problems, was one of them sick, and so on. At last I said, "But weren't you supposed to pick up the groceries?" Well, I won't even try to describe my thoughts and feelings after Katherine explained, "Oh, Mom, we were just too tired to get the groceries. All we wanted to do was get home."

You can well believe that we had a little discussion about responsibility after I blurted, "Well, welcome to the club! Every woman, wife, and mom goes to the grocery store tired!" And it's true that we shop when we're tired. But the shopping needs to be done, which is why we are responsible in that area. Because others in the family depend on us to care for the meals, we have learned to be faithful and carry through on that responsibility.

And by the way, today both my Katherine and Courtney are excellent and super-responsible shoppers...and everything else. They've learned the great value of being responsible.

Now on to this stunning quality which so reflects Jesus. As you move through this chapter keep in mind that, by definition, a responsible woman (young or old) is one who is capable of being trusted to do or finish something. She is competent and reliable. Others can depend on her to do *what* she says she'll do, and to do it *when* she says she'll do it. If someone gives her a task, there are no worries about her or the task. They can count on her to complete it. She'll take care of it. Consider it done!

Jesus Shows You the Way

Well, Jessica is in for another dose of Jesus this week. And would you believe it? The teacher is going to talk about responsibility and how Jesus could be counted on to do and be what was asked and required of Him.

We're on the move again as we look at the character qualities Jesus modeled in His life. For sure if you want to be Christlike, then you'll need to be responsible. Jesus perfectly fits the definitions above...and more! He was totally reliable, fully dependable, and was completely trusted by the Father. And you can put all your trust in Him too.

Who's Number One?

What's behind responsibility? One aspect of this character trait comes from the heart: A responsible person is concerned for others. Jesus was the most responsible person who ever walked the face of the earth. Only Jesus, of all the people who have ever lived, perfectly fulfilled every task and every responsibility that was ever handed to Him.

Jesus was responsible for His disciples—Jesus' band of men was made up of simple and uneducated laborers. They worked hard at their jobs. In fact, they left their jobs to follow and assist Jesus. But Jesus was perfectly and fully responsible for them. He cared for them, saw to their needs, helped pay their taxes, taught them, prayed for them, and prepared them for the day when He would no longer be with them. What do you learn about responsibility from the following verse?

> *While I was with them, I protected them and kept them safe by that name you gave me. None has been lost except the one doomed to destruction so that Scripture would be fulfilled* (John 17:12).

The disciples were kept under Jesus' protection and He lost none of them. And you can fully trust Him too and depend on Him for your eternal life. He affirmed this on another occasion when He said, "I give them eternal life, and they shall never perish; no one can snatch them out of my hand" (John 10:28).

A question for your heart: Responsibility cares for and about others. It looks out for them. But that's not what we saw at the beginning of this chapter when Jessica's choice to sleep in led to bad consequences. It was obvious she was busy looking out for Number One—herself!

Because of Jessica's lack of responsibility, others were adversely affected. Her parents at home had to constantly nag her. Her brother and sisters were deprived of a peaceful, enjoyable breakfast and instead had to endure the tension created by the fact Jessica was running late. Even a bus driver and a busload of high school students were forced to wait as Jessica came running late to catch the bus.

Now for the big question for your heart: Whose interests are you busy looking out for? If you answered "Mine," take time now to write out three or four things you plan to do about taking your eyes off yourself and turning them onto Jesus and others. And even if you didn't answer "Mine," go ahead and write out a few ways you can improve on watching out for others.

—

—

—

—

Jesus was responsible about the future—As a person responsible for countless people, Jesus made plans for the future. He knew there would come a day when He would physically leave earth and return to heaven. So as His time on earth grew shorter and shorter, He lived by a master plan for securing a successful future for all His children, including you. What was His plan for spreading His message after He returned to heaven? Underline His plan and His purpose as seen in the verses below.

> *Jesus went up on a mountainside and called to him those he wanted, and they came to him. He appointed twelve—designating them apostles— that they might be with him and that he might send them out to preach* (Mark 3:13-14).

A responsible person knows what is worth having— what is worth planning for, saving for, securing, and passing on to others. Jesus' plan was to pass on the truth of His message of salvation to a select group of men. Then when He was gone, they in turn would pass it on to others.

A question for your heart: What do you desire for yourself and your growth in the next year or two? Try to make a list of your dreams. Then, with a calendar in hand—and your ever-faithful pen—sketch out a master plan. Just put down some key steps you need to take to move forward. And then get moving, just a small step at a time. Following a master plan will help you become more responsible as you move toward your future.

For example, suppose you have to raise money for a school band trip, or senior trip, or some other cool activity. Getting the money you need starts with setting a goal and then determining what steps you need to take to make it happen. Or maybe you hope to go to college or junior college after high school. That means you need to talk with your parents, start researching colleges, find out about scholarship opportunities, take the SAT exam, and get recommendations from teachers and church and community leaders. Or maybe you want to get a job after high school. Do you know what you're good at? What you like to do? Where your abilities shine? What skills you need to improve? Once again, getting successful results means getting started right now. Write down your goal and the small steps you need to take to reach it—then get going!

And here's another hint for how to grow more responsible. Make a list of the responsibilities you have right now. For instance, you're responsible for your room—or your half of a room if you happen to share it with your sister. So own it! And you're responsible for your schoolwork. So own it! And you're responsible to do the chores assigned to you as a family member. So own them! The more you use to-do lists to help you, the better. You'll surprise yourself by the very real progress you start making toward your goals. And the progress that will give you the most satisfaction is growing more like Jesus as you grow more responsible.

Jesus was responsible to provide—As you already know, Jesus knew from the beginning that He would eventually leave this world. So He chose His men. Then He trained them during the three years that remained before His death. Yet He knew that brief time of training wasn't going to be enough. The disciples would also need Jesus' strength and wisdom even after Jesus returned to heaven. So Jesus promised to send someone just like Him to continue the training, to empower them, to be with them, and to help them be faithful and responsible in all that would be asked of them. As you read the promise Jesus made to His disciples, notice how long the "Helper" or "advocate"—the Holy Spirit—would be with them, as well as with all believers. Also mark the purpose of the Helper.

> *I will ask the Father, and He will give you another Helper, that He may be with you forever* (John 14:16 NASB).

A question for your heart: You probably know a little about your physical, mental, and emotional limits. And you probably at times find yourself stretched too thin by the many demands that are part of your daily life. Hopefully you haven't been like Jessica, who became overwhelmed by the many hats she has to wear and totally gave up on being responsible. She wasn't looking to the resources that were available to her. Fortunately, Jesus knows that you are limited as to what you, as one person, can do. So Jesus has sent another person, a helper, the Holy Spirit, who is always present and always available to help you be more responsible. The catch is that you have to be obedient to "walk in the Spirit" (Galatians 5:16). That means to cooperate with Him. That's your part in making responsibility happen.

So when you have more tasks than time or energy, give thanks to Jesus. He has sent the Holy Spirit, who will give you "the fruit of the Spirit." Galatians 5:22-23 describes this fruit we can enjoy in our lives:

love	joy	peace
forbearance	kindness	goodness
faithfulness	gentleness	self-control

Can you pinpoint one or two of these Christlike qualities that need attention in your life? Circle them, put them on your prayer list as well as your daily to-do list, and make them goals you can pursue. The Holy Spirit will help you to cultivate these qualities and reflect the heart and character of Jesus. Walking by God's Spirit will help you fulfill your responsibilities God's way—in a way that honors Jesus.

Guidelines for Responsibility

We've spent a lot of time talking about God's will. So, by now you certainly know that it is God's will that you be responsible. It's no secret. Just what does that mean?

A responsible young woman is informed—Responsibility

means doing the right thing, at the right time, in the right way. That means you need to know what the right thing is. How can you know that? It's right in God's Word. That makes reading, studying, and learning what's in the Bible a key to doing God's will. It is the Word of God that shows us the way to God. As 2 Timothy 3:15 says, "The holy Scriptures...are able to make you wise for salvation through faith in Christ Jesus." Then, as you read your Bible, you'll discover God's responsibilities for you—both today as a young woman, and in the future as you continue to follow Him through the years.

A responsible young woman is obedient—Is your pen handy? Underline what God has given to you according to 2 Peter 1:3-4:

> *His divine power has given us everything we need for life and godliness through our knowledge of him who called us by his own glory and goodness.*

If God has given us all this—everything we need to live for Him—shouldn't we obey? God is offering you an abundant, victorious life...if you will do what He says to do.

A responsible young woman is growing in faith—For your own good, what does God ask of you in 2 Peter 3:18?

> *Grow in the grace and knowledge of our Lord and Savior Jesus Christ.*

The New Testament is filled with commands, exhortations, admonitions, and encouragement for Christians to grow spiritually mature. It is this maturity that will give you a strong foundation and knowledge of the things of God so you'll know God's will. As in all things, the road to spiritual maturity passes right through the Bible.

Reflecting the Heart of Jesus

Wow—being responsible! That's really out there. But aren't you glad you can look to Jesus? He fulfilled all His responsibilities to the very end, to the very last responsibility—going to the cross to pay the penalty for sin. This was indeed the ultimate act of responsibility for all time. Jesus sacrificed Himself as a ransom for our sins. The fulfillment of His responsibilities to the Father took Him to the cross.

Now, God is not asking you to die for Him. No, He's asking you to *live* for Him, to be a living sacrifice (see Romans 12:1). Jesus possessed a heart of obedience that made Him responsible. And He wants this for you too.

A wonderful scripture says, "Whoever can be trusted with very little can also be trusted with much" (Luke 16:10). That's how responsibility is lived out. So focus on living out the big message in this little saying:

> Let me do the thing that ought to be
>   done,
> When it ought to be done,
> As it ought to be done,
> Whether I like to do it or not.[7]

When you are responsible to faithfully carry out your duties and obligations at home, at school, and in your community—to do the things that ought to be done, God helps you to grow. And then He gives you more ways to serve Him and more ways to be like Him. He delights in your commitment and obedience to Him. These are powerful expressions of your love for Him. So be faithful to fulfill your responsibilities today, just for today. And then wake up again tomorrow and do the same. This kind of commitment is how you can live as Jesus lived.

My friend, if you truly desire to reflect the heart of Jesus, then nurture a heart that is responsible to obey God and follow the example of His Son, the Lord Jesus.

∼ A Prayer to Pray ∼

Dear Lord Jesus, I do love You, and my heart's desire is to become more like You. As I learn about responsibility, I want my attitudes and actions to demonstrate that I belong to You. Thank You for the gift of Your Holy Spirit, who will help me to be responsible as I live for You, and as I seek to live like You. Amen.

Want to Know More About...
Being Responsible?

Read these verses and note what they say about being responsible...and irresponsible.

Proverbs 25:13—

Proverbs 25:19—

Proverbs 26:6—

Proverbs 26:13—

Scan Jesus' parable in Matthew 25:14-30. Why did the man in verses 24-25 fail to be responsible?

How did Jesus evaluate this man's character in verse 26?

Think about your work habits. What messages do these verses have for you?

Proverbs 31:13—

Ephesians 2:10—

1 Corinthians 15:58—

Which of these verses were your favorites or the most challenging, and why?

9

★ ★ ★ ★

A Servant
May I Help You?

Jessica was so thrilled that her birthday this year was going to fall on Saturday. Why? The Edwards household had a birthday tradition that went way back. Well, at least as far back as Jessica and her sisters and brother could remember. On your birthday, you could stay in your PJ's all day (well, unless it was a school day). You got to choose the menu for your favorite breakfast, lunch, and dinner. On top of all this, you were absolutely not allowed to make your bed or do any work. And best of all, you were to be waited on by the other family members all day long. Sweet!

This may be a part of the "Birthday Special" at home, but with glee, Jessica tried to exploit the "being waited on" thing every day and every chance she got. Once in a while when she was able to catch another family member off guard, she could ask that person to go get something for her or do something that made her day go better. And, of course, she could always intimidate her little sister Jenny into being her servant or personal slave. Sweet again!

"Being served is much better than serving" was the motto Jessica lived by. Therefore she was always on the lookout for ways to be served. In fact, Jessica expended more energy looking for ways to avoid serving than it would take to actually just do the serving!

These were some of the thoughts running through Jessica's mind as she sat in her chair waiting for this week's Bible study lesson to begin. "Where is my snack?" she muttered, looking around to see why her friend Wendy was taking so long to bring her favorite chips. (Jessica had hinted to Wendy that she would like to have a snack before the class started. And Wendy had jumped up to get the snack—unbelievable!) As Wendy handed Jessica a bag of chips and settled into her chair next to Jessica, the youth leader began this week's lesson about Jesus.

Little did poor Jessica realize she was about to learn that Jesus was the perfect, amazing, willing, loving servant. The youth pastor opened the evening by reading Matthew 20:28:

> *The Son of Man did not come to be served, but to serve, and to give his life as a ransom for many.*

Then he went on to say, "One thing about this truth that touches my heart is that the book of Matthew shows us Jesus as the Christ, the Messiah, the King, and King of kings. And yet we read that serving was a strong quality in Jesus' life—a priority and a way of life for Him."

"Oh, dear!" Jessica gulped. "I think I'm really in for a makeover, whether I want it or not!"

Jesus Shows You the Way

When you think of the "super servants" in your life, who comes to mind? Do you know any Wendys? Think of those you know, and if possible, list some of them here.

Now write a few words that describe what these people do or have done for you that demonstrates a servant spirit.

Serving is a unique and beautiful quality that is also a "spiritual gift" given by God to some people in the church, the body of Christ. As you read the verses below, note or circle the gifts listed, along with the service they provide.

> *We have different gifts, according to the grace given us. If a man's gift is prophesying, let him use it in proportion to his faith. If it is serving, let him serve; if it is teaching, let him teach* (Romans 12:6-7).

For those who are gifted by God to serve, serving seems like their second nature. They love helping others and somehow seem to know exactly what to do to help them. But what does the Bible say to those who don't have God's gift of serving? Find the answer in the verse below and write it out.

> *You, my brothers, were called to be free. But do not use your freedom to indulge the sinful nature; rather, serve one another in love* (Galatians 5:13).

As you, along with Jessica, consider today's quality of serving and being a servant, give praise to God that Jesus, the Messiah, the Savior of the world, came first as a lowly servant. Then open your heart and eyes to see how the greatest man—and servant—who ever lived modeled what it means to serve.

Who Should I Serve First?

I know your days are already packed with people and responsibilities. You probably get started early at the blare of your alarm clock—or when Mom tries to wake you up. With all that you have to do, you may find yourself wondering, *If serving others is so important, where do I start? Who should I serve first?*

The key to answering this question is setting the priorities you are given in these verses:

*"Love the Lord your God with all your heart
and with all your soul and with all your mind."
This is the first and greatest commandment*
(Matthew 22:37-38).

What—or who—does this passage say is to be your
first priority?

How is this priority to be lived out?

If you're not careful, your service can become completely focused on people. Maybe you enjoy it. Maybe
people notice you. Maybe people thank you and express
their appreciation. Maybe it feels good to help others.
But then one day you realize you've forgotten about your
call to serve God. Jesus spoke to this priority. Loving and
serving God is the most important thing a Christian can do.
It's to be your first priority. Here's what the Bible teaches
regarding your service to Him. If you can, underline where
your focus is to be and what God's "aim" is for you.

*An unmarried woman or virgin is [to be] con-
cerned about the Lord's affairs: Her aim is to
be devoted to the Lord in both body and spirit*
(1 Corinthians 7:34).

You Cannot Serve Two Masters

In Jesus' day the religious leaders loved their worldly possessions, their things, their stuff. One day as they were listening to Jesus tell a parable about good stewardship (Luke 16:1-12), Jesus ended with this truth:

> *No servant can serve two masters. Either he will hate the one and love the other, or he will be devoted to the one and despise the other. You cannot serve both God and Money* [or the things money can buy] (Luke 16:13).

To begin, what fact of life is stated by Jesus?

What are the two options presented here for your loyalty and love?

What struggle is described between these two options?

Where is your focus, or what is your "master"? And what changes do you need to make?

Obsession with money and possessions can take your eyes off Jesus. Your clothes, your social status at school, even your friends can easily become your master. What does Jesus say about your priorities in Matthew 6:33?

Seek first the kingdom of God and His righteousness (NKJV).

God wants—and deserves—the Number One slot in your life. What can you do to make sure you are putting Him first? List one or two actions you can take this week.

—

—

A question for your heart: How can you tell if you're beginning to lose your focus on Jesus or starting to serve things and stuff instead of serving Jesus and His people? A few honest answers to a handful of questions will point to the obvious.

Circle how often you think about the latest styles in clothes, what to wear to school, or what others will think of your appearance.

All the time   A lot   About once a day

Does your desire for social status ever get in the way of serving God? Or put another way, does it embarrass you to speak out for Christ or be involved in some Christian activities or be seen helping someone with a need?

About how much time do you spend each day taking care of your clothes, your hair, your hobbies, your stuff, your music?

Is it easy or hard for you to give some of your allowance or babysitting money to support missionaries or meet some need among God's people? In a few words, explain your answer. Tell why it's easy or hard.

What was your response the last time someone had a need?

These are some tough questions, aren't they? You are growing up in a privileged society. Do you realize how blessed you are? But that blessing can become a curse if money, possessions, clothes, cars, or popularity get in the way of serving God and His people. Once again, examine your heart. If there's a problem with "mammon" or your-money or stuff, spend some time with Jesus. Talk it over with Him. Look for ways to turn your priorities around. Remember, if you can't let go of your possessions, you don't own them; they own you!

What, Me Serve?

Many people all over the world, Christian and non-Christian, past and present, agree Jesus was a great person.

What did He do that has caused people around the globe to acknowledge He was the greatest man of all times, the greatest man who ever lived? Jesus never wrote a book. He never commanded an army of soldiers. He never moved people to revolt. In fact, He never even traveled more than a few days' journey by foot from His birthplace. So what was the powerful quality in His life that made Him stand out so much?

In a very few words, He served others.

But serving others was not important to Jesus' disciples. Can you believe it? After all the time—three years!—they spent with the greatest servant who ever lived, they missed it. That's because their eyes and aims were somewhere else. They were watching the people and leaders around them instead of watching Jesus. As a result, they concluded that greatness came from being a "lord" over others. So now Jesus needed to teach His disciples a new lesson. His ministry on earth was almost over, and they needed to get "greatness" in perspective. So,

> *Jesus called them together and said, "You know that the rulers of the Gentiles lord it over them, and their high officials exercise authority over them. Not so with you. Instead, whoever wants to become great among you must be your servant, and whoever wants to be first must be your slave—just as the Son of Man did not come to be served, but to serve, and to give his life as a ransom for many"* (Matthew 20:25-28).

What two kinds of people does Jesus contrast?

How is Jesus and His ministry described?

What did Jesus say was the key to greatness?

Jesus' disciples had been affected by their culture. And little has changed these 2000 years later. In the same way that our lives are filled with cruel and mean people, their lives were too. No one wanted to serve. So they had servants do the serving. For the disciples, serving and helping others was the farthest thing from their minds. They wanted to be great! And to them, greatness was defined as lordship, not servanthood.

Like these 12 men, you are surrounded by a culture that is self-centered and wants to be served rather than serve others. As you look around I'm sure you can see that most of the kids you know are selfish and self-absorbed. They are lazy when it comes to serving others. And (like Jessica) they are constantly thinking of ways to be served or get others to do their work. Like the disciples, you may be having a hard time dealing with the concept of serving. It simply does not compute!

But look to Jesus. He came to earth with a different lifestyle and a radical life-message. He defined true greatness as serving others. And then He lived out the definition. His mission was to serve others and to give His very life away. That's what He did. And you are to follow His example, to reflect Him. You are to develop a servant's heart and help others by taking care of their needs.

A question for your heart: Is this concept new to you? And are you struggling with even wanting to serve? If so, decide that you will do something whenever you see a need or something that needs to get done. Decide you won't wait to be asked to help or wait for someone else to do it. Make it a goal to volunteer to serve at home, school, and church. Open your heart. Open your eyes. And open your hands. Do what needs to be done. Be like Jesus! Be a loving servant. Once again, what example does the ideal woman in Proverbs 31 live out? How do you see her serving?

> *She reaches out her hands to the needy* (verse 20 NASB).

Your Attitude Is Showing

Do you remember Jesus' friends, the two sisters Mary and Martha? We met them in our chapter on friendship. Poor Martha always comes off as the less spiritual sister. Let's quickly review their story: Jesus was traveling and *a certain woman named Martha welcomed Him into her house. And she had a sister called Mary, who also sat at Jesus' feet and heard His word. But Martha was distracted with much serving, and she approached Him and said, "Lord, do You not care that my sister has left me to serve alone? Therefore tell her to help me." And Jesus answered and said to her, "Martha, Martha, you are worried and troubled about many things. But one thing is needed, and Mary has chosen that good part, which will not be taken away from her"* (Luke 10:38-42 NKJV).

Jesus' message to Martha was on multiple levels. But please don't miss His point about serving. As we've been learning, serving others is a good thing. And Martha was a true servant. She loved Jesus and opened her home to Him. She delighted in cooking for Him and serving Him and the disciples.

But poor Martha also shows us that we can do our service with a wrong attitude. Go back and notice and underline the words she spoke that gave away her attitude.

Can't you just sense her attitude? She was running around (literally spinning about) serving. Plus she was upset that Mary had stopped helping her and was sitting— yes, sitting—by Jesus to hear His teaching. Well, Martha finally broke...and she broke into Jesus' time of ministry with accusations against both the Lord and Mary.

You see, Martha was resentful of her sister. She gritted her teeth for as long as she could take it. Then she stormed out of the kitchen, lashed out at Jesus, and accused Him of not caring. Then she lit into her sister for shirking her duties. Martha would have been better off not serving than serving with a bad attitude. ·

A question for your heart: Do you ever find yourself with a "Martha attitude"? You're serving, but resenting every minute of it! You agreed to serve, or were told to, but your heart just isn't in it. You would rather be the one being served. When this happens, remember Martha. Realize your problem and refuse to take your frustrations out on others. Instead, take a break. Step back. Admit your bad attitude. Ask Jesus to give you His servant heart for the work in front of you. Then, in the future, evaluate service opportunities before you say *yes*.

Don't agree to serve if you're doing it for the wrong reasons—reasons such as peer pressure, expectation, pride, guilt, or a sense of duty. Your primary reason for serving is Jesus. He served you in the greatest way possible when He gave His life for you. And He wants you to follow His example, to be like Him. As He told His disciples after He had stooped and washed their dirty feet, "I have given you an example, that you should do as I have done to you" (John 13:15 NKJV).

If Jesus, God in flesh, the King of kings and Lord of lords, the Messiah, the Christ, the Savior of mankind, was willing to serve, even to the point of washing feet, shouldn't you be willing to serve as well?

Reflecting the Heart of Jesus

If you are a young woman who wants to develop character qualities that are like Jesus', by now you probably realize that growing a servant spirit is a must. Following in the steps of Jesus and reflecting Him requires a decision to focus your attention on developing the heart attitude of a servant. And this stunning quality begins at home with your family, right under your own roof. God has given you the assignment of being a servant to your parents, starting with His instruction that you "obey your parents" (Ephesians 6:1). Then you are to follow His command in Galatians 5:13 to "serve one another," which includes not only your parents, but your brothers and sisters...and everyone else.

Serving. It's a simple and noble assignment. And it is perhaps the most obvious sign of Jesus in you. When you serve others, your service will become an awesome reflection of the heart of your Savior, the greatest servant who ever lived, the One who set the standard for service when He...

> ...served others whether it was convenient or not,
>
> ...served others whether they deserved it or not,
>
> ...served others whether they thanked Him or not,
>
> ...served others with sacrificial love, and
>
> ...served you by giving His life as a ransom for your soul.

~ *A Prayer to Pray* ~

O Lord, give me a heart of joy so I can follow in Your steps and gladly serve others. I need Your help! When my heart grows cold or gets tired of serving, remind me of Yourself and how Your holy hands washed dirty feet. I want to become like You—I want to serve the needs of others. Please help me! Amen, and thank You.

Want to Know More About...
Being a Servant?

What do these verses tell you about serving and being a servant?

Romans 12:11—

Galatians 5:13—

Ephesians 6:7—

Colossians 3:23-24—

Read Acts 6:1-3. What was the problem, and how was it solved?

What kind of people were chosen to serve?

You've already met these women, but read Luke 10:38-42 in your Bible.

Describe the scene and why Mary and Martha were serving.

Describe Mary's service.

Describe Martha's service.

What did Jesus say was wrong about Martha's service?

In general, what is your attitude when you are serving others?

Which of these verses were your favorites or the most challenging, and why?

10

★ ★ ★ ★

Thankful

I Appreciate You

Enter the drama queen, with hand on forehead, speaking with a quivering, hurt, and forlorn tone of voice. "Why, oh why, can't I have a new pair of designer jeans? Everyone else will be wearing the latest. Unless I show up with mine on the first day of classes, I'll be the laughingstock of the school!" (Never mind her "old" jeans had cost over $100!)

Jessica's family was a middle-class family with two working parents who struggled to provide even the basics for their girls and their son. Jessica's older sister, Ruth, was attending a state college, which was quite expensive. Then there were Jessica's braces and her music lessons. And being on the swim team cost money for trips and events. Jessica was fortunate to have two loving parents who were trying to give her some of the things that make for a normal life. But Jessica failed to be grateful for what she did have. In fact, she wanted more. More of everything!

As Jessica stomped off to her room to get ready for church and the next youth group study, she made a very foolish statement that she would regret for some time—especially after that evening's lesson on the life of Jesus. She blurted out, "Why couldn't I have been born in a family like Billie Jo's? I bet she'll show up on the first day of school in some cool new designer jeans!"

A Reality Check

I recently received a letter from a missionary in an Eastern European country who shared about her ministry to young teen girls in an orphanage. Evidently most of these teenagers had no parents, or they had been abandoned by their parents for one reason or another and put into the care of this orphanage.

The girls had very few personal possessions and no books or reading materials of their own. The missionary related how, each day, the girls could hardly wait for her to read to them out of her copy of one of my teen books. Thirty girls and one book! The missionary was writing to let me know how thankful the girls were that I had written that book…and that she had a copy of it.

Wow—what a reality check! This sure puts Jessica's cry for designer jeans into perspective, doesn't it? As Jessica arrives for yet another lesson on the life of Jesus, the teacher continues to walk the class through the gallery of character qualities Jesus possessed. They are now about to look at Jesus' thankful attitude.

Jesus Shows You the Way

Praise, thankfulness, and gratitude should be a regular part of our everyday life as Christians. Just think about it—we have so much! But unfortunately our well-to-do society has dulled our sensitivity to God's grace and gracious provision. It's too bad it takes a letter from a missionary in a country where Christians are persecuted and are forced to go without the things we take for granted to wake us up to acknowledge even the smallest blessings we enjoy as God's children.

Thankfulness. It's a truly amazing quality because, as the Son of God, Jesus created and possessed everything. Yet He never failed to demonstrate a thankful spirit to His heavenly Father. As we spend time now looking at thankfulness, pause to thank God for "His indescribable gift" of His Son Jesus, our Savior (2 Corinthians 9:15).

Be Thankful for Others

Jesus' cousin, John the Baptist, was very popular among the people of Israel. Large crowds followed him. They listened to him preach, and answered his call for repentance. At the peak of John's popularity, Jesus, the Messiah, came to the Jordan River, where John was conducting his ministry. How did John react to Jesus' visit, especially now that many people were turning their attention to Jesus and following Him? As you read John's response, underline what impresses you most about John's attitude toward his famous cousin.

> *I am not the Christ but am sent ahead of him...*
> *He must become greater; I must become less*
> (John 3:28,30).

John also expressed joy, thankfulness, and appreciation that Jesus was the Messiah and had at last arrived. He said, "Joy is mine, and it is now complete" (verse 29).

Most people have trouble being glad about the success of others. As you know all too well, if you're not careful, you can become jealous of others who are more gifted and can do a better job than you. You can become threatened by their abilities and resent the attention they receive for their successes. And if you're like me, you can think of a time (or two!) when you were just a little bit envious of a fellow student or teammate—or even a brother or sister— who excelled.

Well, like John the Baptist, we must realize that these people are, by God's design, a part of our lives. They give us an opportunity to grow in thankfulness as we recognize great talent and dedication in others and learn to rejoice with them. And, also like John, we have a choice about whether we want to support or be unhappy about their achievements. John realized that he was witnessing one who was destined for great things. Therefore he thanked and praised God for Jesus. And he pointed others to Jesus. Then, instead of standing in the way of Jesus' ministry, John stepped out of the way so others would follow Jesus.

A question for your heart: Are there people in your school or even your family who have wonderful talents and abilities you don't possess? Are you feeling threatened? Jealous? Bitter? Both Jesus and John show you a better way. Think of several things you could do to reflect Jesus in your relationship with these individuals. Could you tell them what a great job they are doing? Could you write or text them a note congratulating them on a win, or a good game, or an award? Could you pray for them to continue to excel?

If you're having trouble thinking of a positive response, follow John's example: Step aside. Or, see if there is anything you can do to help those individuals. Speak well of them to others. And be thankful to God for their excellence and their abilities.

Express Your Praise of Others

I love how Jesus and John complimented and praised each other. See for yourself as you fast-forward now in John the Baptist's ministry. John had introduced Jesus to the people as the One who would bring judgment with His coming (Matthew 3:11-12). Later, when John was put in prison, he heard that Jesus was healing the sick instead of bringing judgment (as John had thought the Messiah would). He wondered, "Was Jesus really the One, the Messiah?" In the hopes of resolving his confusion, John sent several of his own disciples to ask Jesus if He was truly the Messiah. In response, Jesus sent John's disciples back to him as eyewitnesses of His many miracles.

Maybe John was a little discouraged. After all, he had been preaching for only one year, and now he was in prison! As John's disciples left Jesus and returned to John, Jesus spoke to the crowd around Him. After asking them what they were expecting of John, Jesus praised John. Circle some of the compliments Jesus gave concerning John:

> *What did you go out to see? A prophet? Yes, I tell*
> *you, and more than a prophet. This is the one*
> *about whom it is written: "I will send my mes-*
> *senger ahead of you, who will prepare your way*
> *before you." I tell you the truth: Among those*
> *born of women there has not risen anyone*
> *greater than John the Baptist* (Matthew 11:9-11).

What beautiful words of praise and encouragement! Hopefully John's disciples told him what they had seen Jesus do and heard Him say in praise of John, their teacher.

John the Baptist was definitely special. He was the one chosen by God to serve as a messenger who heralded the coming Messiah. Jesus wanted the people to know how unique John was. He wanted them to know how thankful He was for John. And He wanted to make sure they didn't forget about John.

Being thankful for those who have helped you get to where you are in your life today is an important part of an attitude of thankfulness. That's what Jesus shows us. He was thankful that the Father had sent John as His herald, His messenger. Unless someone had preceded the King to tell people of His coming, how would they know that He was coming?

A question for your heart: It's easy to forget what others have done for you and sacrificed and contributed to help you get to where you are today. Maybe it's your parents, a former teacher, a mentor, a coach, or a youth leader at church who showed you the ropes when you were new or just beginning to grow. Or maybe someone encouraged you when you weren't sure you could go on. Sure, maybe some of these people were just doing their job. But that shouldn't keep you from saying "Thank you" for their help and support. The disciples had Jesus. Timothy and Titus had Paul. Mark had Peter. Mary had Elizabeth. And God has given you someone too.

Who do you have? Who are you grateful for? As you think of them, express your thankfulness for them—first to God, then to them, and then to anyone else who will listen!

Be Thankful for Everything

After being rejected by the people in Nazareth (Matthew 4:13), Jesus moved His headquarters to the town of Capernaum. He performed many wondrous miracles in and around this area. Wouldn't you think the people would joyfully receive Him as the Messiah? Oh no! They were numb toward Him. What did Jesus do? How did He respond? He rebuked them for their rejection (11:20-24). But then He did something quite unexpected. Rather than being downcast, He offered up thanks or praise to His Father:

> *At that time Jesus said, "I praise you, Father, Lord of heaven and earth, because you have hidden these things from the wise and learned, and revealed them to little children"* (Matthew 11:25).

A question for your heart: Has anything ever happened in your life that didn't make sense? Maybe you couldn't understand how a loving God could allow something like that to happen to you or someone you love. Well, you are not alone. Most people find themselves in circumstances that are difficult or impossible to understand. Rather than question the "Father, Lord of heaven and earth" with your whys, take a page out of Jesus' life and be thankful even for the hard things in your life. Think about this instruction from the Bible:

> *Give thanks in all circumstances, for this is God's will for you in Christ Jesus* (1 Thessalonians 5:18).

According to this verse, what are you to be thankful for, and why? Jot down a few answers. Then stop and do what the verse says—give thanks to God.

Be Thankful God Hears Your Prayers

Jesus had the 12 disciples, but He also had some special friends—Lazarus and his two sisters, Mary and Martha. Jesus had visited their home many times. We've met these three siblings before, but this time we're going to focus on something different. We're going to look at an encounter with them that caused Jesus to verbally give thanks to God.

As Jesus neared the end of His three years of earthly ministry, He received news that His friend Lazarus was sick. By the time Jesus arrived on the scene, Lazarus was dead and had been in his grave four days. After meeting with the sisters, Jesus ordered Lazarus's tomb to be opened. Everyone was shocked as they thought about what they would see…and smell! As they removed the stone from the tomb, Jesus offered up this prayer of thanksgiving:

> *Father, I thank you that you have heard me. I knew that you always hear me, but I said this for the benefit of the people standing here, that they may believe that you sent me* (John 11:41-42).

What was Jesus thankful for?

Jesus and the Father were never out of touch. Therefore there was no need for our Lord to pray at all, or to pray out loud in public. But here Jesus openly and publicly thanked His Father. Why? So all could hear. Jesus wanted those present at the grave site—and us today—to give thanks that God is always at our side and always hears us when we pray.

Reflecting a Thankful Spirit

To the end of His life and ministry on earth, Jesus continued to offer up prayers of thanks and gratitude to the Father. In what is often referred to as His "high priestly prayer," which He prayed before His betrayal and crucifixion, Jesus…

...thanked the Father that He could obtain eternal life for all believers (John 17:2).

...thanked the Father for giving Him the disciples (verses 6-7).

...thanked the Father that believers had heard and obeyed what He had spoken (verse 8).

Then, with a heart of thankfulness, Jesus turned His focus on the cross and His death. How could Jesus be thankful for the cross? And what was the reason for this grateful attitude? He knew the Father was in absolute control. He knew everything was going according to God's divine plan.

Is yours a heart filled with thanksgiving? Is there any reason you don't exhibit more of Jesus' thankful attitude? For instance,

Maybe you don't know Jesus and are facing an unknown future without confidence. Ask God to grant you His grace to receive Jesus Christ as your Savior and give you the gift of eternal life. Then you too can be abundantly thankful (Ephesians 2:8-9).

Or maybe you are a Christian but you've forgotten how hopeless your life was before you knew and belonged to Jesus. There is no greater gift than the gift of salvation. And, as you should do with any gift, you should say "Thank you." You can do it now! Pause for a moment and thank God for His unspeakable gift in Jesus Christ. Then purpose in your heart to say "Thank you"—constantly!

Reflecting the Heart of Jesus

Everyone loves Thanksgiving Day. Traditionally a Thanksgiving Day celebration includes lots of food and family. But it also includes the giving of thanks and expressing gratitude to God for the harvest of His bounty and provision. But praise and thanksgiving shouldn't be reserved for just one special designated day. It should be a regular part of every day. You can thank God before you get out of bed. Thank Him for each meal. Thank Him for family, friends, a good church, and, of course, for His provision. Keep going, and thank God for the people He places in your path. And go one more step and express your thanks to those people as well. You can never say "Thank you" enough to friends, church leaders, and especially to immediate family. And above all else, thanks should flow from your heart and lips to God for His gift of Jesus.

A Prayer to Pray

O Lord, I want to thank You with a heart of gratitude. You have blessed me abundantly! You have provided the forgiveness of my sins. And You have given me the gift of my family and church. Thank You, thank You, thank You, dear Lord, for these things and so many more! Amen.

Want to Know More About...
Being Thankful?

Read Luke 17:12-19. What was the request of the men who approached Jesus, and how did Jesus respond?

What happened in verse 15?

What did Jesus ask in verse 17?

What does this indicate about thanking God for His every work in your life?

Read these verses in your Bible and note how they advise you to be thankful and live with a thankful spirit.

Psalm 106:1—

Psalm 147:7—

Ephesians 5:20—

Colossians 3:15—

1 Thessalonians 5:18—

Which of these verses were your favorites or the most challenging, and why?

11

★ ★ ★ ★

Truthful

To Be Honest with You...

I'm sure you have heard of "little white lies." This is the very popular concept that excuses a lie if it's not really that bad. If it's not a big black ugly lie, but just a little white one, then supposedly it's an acceptable lie. This attitude was a part of Jessica's daily life. Besides having learned to turn graciousness on and off, she had bought into the idea that telling little white lies was okay, and she had developed it into an art form!

For instance, just the other day, Jessica was confronted with a difficult situation. Her friend Wendy was writing a paper for her English class at Roosevelt High. Wendy was a great friend, always willing to help, and a very nice person. And there she was, asking Jessica to please read her paper and give her some feedback. No problem. Jessica was happy to help. But then Jessica found herself in a tough spot. Wendy's English paper was awful! Even Jessica could tell that.

So what should she do? Well, for sure Jessica didn't want to hurt Wendy's feelings. And for sure she didn't want to risk losing Wendy as a friend. So Jessica decided to tell her friend that her paper was okay. "Good job, Wendy!" At the same time, Jessica told herself this wasn't a big deal. She wasn't telling Wendy a big fat lie—only a little white one.

Well, unfortunately Wendy ended up getting a D on her paper. So you can imagine her confusion and disappointment—after all, hadn't Jessica told her the paper was okay? Right then, Jessica learned firsthand that even a little white lie can be harmful and have negative consequences.

The next day, a girl named Debra asked Jessica if she could sit with her at lunch in the school cafeteria. Jessica in no way wanted to be seen with "Weird Debra" in the cafeteria. So she quickly made up a story about why she wouldn't be eating lunch on this particular day. Rather than acknowledge and deal with her social snobbery, Jessica told a lie about why she couldn't have lunch with a lonely girl who had reached out to her.

Can you imagine how Jessica's heart began to race when her youth pastor opened this week's lesson on the life of Jesus by reading from Ephesians 4:25? There, the apostle Paul wrote, "Laying aside falsehood, speak truth each one of you with his neighbor." As Jessica listened, she realized that even a little white lie was wrong. Jesus' standard for good character was to speak the truth and be truthful at all times. In her heart, Jessica realized she needed to apologize to Wendy. "Oh, boy! Help me, Lord," Jessica prayed.

The Truth About Truth

Have you ever wondered where the concept and reality of truth and truthfulness came from? All things related to truth originated with God. As you read on, note or mark what these verses tell you about God:

God the Father: *"God...does not lie"* (Titus 1:2).

God the Holy Spirit: *"God is spirit, and his worshipers must worship in spirit and in truth"* (John 4:24).

"I will ask the Father, and he will give you another Counselor to be with you forever—the Spirit of truth" (John 14:16-17).

Jesus, the Son of God: *"I am the way and the truth and the life"* (John 14:6).

"The Word became flesh and made his dwelling among us. We have seen his glory, the glory of the One and Only, who came from the Father, full of grace and truth" (John 1:14).

God's Word, the Bible: *"Sanctify them by the truth; your word is truth"* (John 17:17).

We'll look at Jesus' life of truth and His teachings in a minute. But for now, do you realize that telling the truth is included in the Ten Commandments? The ninth commandment says, "You shall not give false testimony against your neighbor" (Exodus 20:16).

Not only does God command us to tell the truth, He also hates lies and lying. As you read the verses that follow, underline God's attitudes and the actions He takes against those who lie:

You destroy those who tell lies; bloodthirsty and deceitful men the LORD abhors (Psalm 5:6).

The LORD detests lying lips, but he delights in men who are truthful (Proverbs 12:22).

And here's a shocking exercise: Read and number the

seven things God says He hates, and underline the ones that deal with lying. Don't forget to circle God's attitudes toward these seven sins.

> *There are six things the LORD hates, seven that are detestable to him: haughty eyes, a lying tongue, hands that shed innocent blood, a heart that devises wicked schemes, feet that are quick to rush into evil, a false witness who pours out lies and a man who stirs up dissension among brothers* (Proverbs 6:16-19).

As a young woman who loves God and wants to follow Him and reflect the awe-inspiring qualities your Savior displayed, commit yourself right now to seeking this virtue of being truthful...just like our Jesus was.

Jesus Shows You the Way

Because Jesus was—and is—the truth, it's a little more difficult to pin down the evidence of this character quality in Him because He simply lived it. He was truth. But there are some things He said that we can take to heart as we endeavor to speak and walk in truth.

A Study in Contrasts

The Jewish scribes and Pharisees, who were the religious leaders of Jesus' day, were very vocal about rejecting Jesus' teachings. During one of those interactions, Jesus gave the following response. As you read along, be sure to mark how Jesus describes the devil:

> *You belong to your father, the devil...He was a*
> *murderer from the beginning, not holding to*
> *the truth, for there is no truth in him. When he*
> *lies, he speaks his native language, for he is a*
> *liar and the father of lies. Yet because I tell the*
> *truth, you do not believe me!* (John 8:44-45).

I hope you noticed the contrasts—the devil versus Christ, and lying versus telling the truth. This is pretty clear, isn't it? And shocking! As one Bible scholar explains, "The attitudes and actions of the Jewish leaders clearly identified them as followers of Satan...They were Satan's tools in carrying out his plans; they spoke the very same language of lies."[8]

A question for your heart: God and His Son, Jesus, make it painstakingly clear that lying has no place in a child of God. To follow God—who hates lying—means you are to tell the truth and refuse to lie. And to believe in Jesus—who is the truth and spoke the truth—means you are to speak only the truth. Do you want to please God? Do you want to live—and speak—as His Son did? Look again at Proverbs 12:22. What is it that pleases God?

> *The LORD detests lying lips, but he delights in*
> *men who are truthful.*

Say What You Mean

Jesus was the Master Teacher. As such He usually taught in a way that there was no chance of misunderstanding or miscommunication. He was straightforward, simple, and clear with the truths He wanted His followers to understand and apply. His message was "Tell the truth!"

Often we are asked questions that are uncomfortable to answer truthfully. Maybe we are trying to hide an act or choice that could really get us into trouble. The next time this happens to you, follow Jesus' command and say what you mean. Don't try to hide the truth with a veiled answer. Remember, a half-truth is still a lie. So be honest. Tell the truth. Say what you mean...and do what you say you'll do or not do. Then others can trust and believe you, and you will never have to try to convince others of your truthfulness.

That's what was happening when Jesus spoke some very practical words in Matthew 5:37 that I recite to myself just about every day: "Simply let your 'Yes' be 'Yes,' and your 'No,' 'No.'"

The practice in Jesus' day—and some people still do this today—was to make an oath or to swear that what you said was the truth. When your *yes* really does mean *yes* and your *no* really does mean *no*, there's no need to ever swear on anyone's grave or in someone's name. There's no need to harp on the fact that what you are saying really is true or that you are speaking honestly. And there's no need to claim that God is your witness. As Christians, we are accountable to God for every word we speak. Therefore we should speak only the truth, and no more.

The Bible to the Rescue!

We've seen some bad news—God hates lying and liars. Well, thankfully there is also some good news that awaits us. The Bible is filled with help and instruction for becoming a young woman who reflects Jesus and His truthfulness. The teachings and commands found on the pages of Scripture tell us how to deal with the age-old problem of choosing whether to tell the truth...or to lie. Look now at several verses that will help you walk and live in truthfulness.

> *Therefore each of you must put off falsehood and speak truthfully to his neighbor* (Ephesians 4:25).

What is it you are to stop doing?

Now write out the second half of this verse. What are you to do instead?

Lying is a choice, and God says, "Make the right choice!" So this verse means you are to choose to have no part in lies and lying. You are to put lying away, to set it aside, to get rid of it, to have nothing to do with it. So out goes the old behavior of lying, and in comes the new behavior— speaking the truth. The apostle Paul, who wrote Ephesians 4:25, was talking about unity among believers in Christ. He knew that lying undermines trust and destroys relationships.

I'm sure you realize that as well—that lying can hurt your friendships, your family, your fellow Christians, and others.

Paul wrote another bit of advice for us about truth. This time he cautions us about how truth is to be communicated.

> *Speaking the truth in love, we will in all things grow up into him who is the Head, that is, Christ* (Ephesians 4:15).

How does Paul say you are to speak the truth?

What is the result of following this command?

Truth is truth, but without love, truth can sometimes come across as harsh, cold, or mean. In the words of British Christian leader and clergyman John Stott, "Truth becomes hard if not softened by love; love becomes soft if it is not strengthened by truth."[9]

A question for your heart: How's your love quotient? Wherever you go and whenever you spend time with anyone—your family, friends, neighbors, classmates at school, or the kids at church—you'll be talking for sure! And if your mouth is open, you should be making every effort to speak the truth and nothing but the truth...and with love. It's a tall order, but it comes directly from God.

So, where is the first place you should begin practicing the art of speaking in love? As with all of the character qualities of Jesus we're learning about in this book, your home is the best place. Begin there to develop the habit of communicating truth with love. And this doesn't just apply to your parents, but also to your brothers and sisters. For instance, tattling is usually not done in love. It's often done out of spite to get others in trouble with your parents or teachers. These verses will help you speak the truth in love to Mom, Dad, your siblings, and everyone. Underline or take note of what you need to do...and not do.

> *The heart of the righteous weighs its answers,*
> *but the mouth of the wicked gushes evil* (Proverbs 15:28).

> *The wise in heart are called discerning, and*
> *pleasant words promote instruction.* (Proverbs 16:23).

As you can see, effort has to be put into speaking the truth with love. Once you learn the how-tos of telling the truth at home, then you're set to do the same with others elsewhere.

Gossip Is Ghastly

Because this book is about being a young woman who reflects the heart of Jesus, I especially wanted to talk about gossip and slander. I've written in several of my books about my own struggles with these two sins that come so easily, so naturally. The key Bible verses and truths that spoke to my heart were specifically directed to women. One of those passages states that the women who serve in the church "are to be women worthy of respect, not *malicious talkers* but temperate and trustworthy in everything" (1 Timothy 3:11). The message is clear and obvious. The women who serve others in the church must not be gossips.

The other life-changing verse says that the women who minister to other women in the church are "to be reverent in the way they live, *not to be slanderers*" (Titus 2:3).

Hmmm. Did you notice the words in both verses that deal with gossip and slander? The message is clear that you and I as women—especially as women who are to reflect Jesus in our behavior—are not to slander or gossip about others. And here's a scary fact: the words *slander* and *slanderer* are used 34 times in the New Testament to describe Satan. That's ghastly! And, as we learned earlier in this chapter, Satan is a liar and the father of lies. He stands for everything that is the opposite of truth.

As I said, I had a problem—a b-i-g problem—with gossip and slander. But thankfully the truths in the Bible came to my rescue. And they will do the same for you as you start seeking Christlikeness in your speech right now. Speaking the truth is a habit that should be learned early, and the sooner the better. With God's help—and your own desire to be more like Jesus—you can master what you say.

Reflecting the Heart of Jesus

Truthfulness is a golden quality. And it's also timeless. It's changeless because it is connected with the changeless character of God. God cannot lie. He has communicated utterly unchangeable truth to you in His Word. And because He is truthful, you can believe everything He says is the truth. And Jesus was also truthful at all times, even in the most difficult situations, regardless of what it cost. He lived out truthfulness on a daily basis, moment by moment, and the Father was glorified by His consistent example.

As a young woman who loves Jesus, I'm sure you want to honor Him with your behavior—and with the words of your mouth. Well, you reflect Him and act like Him when you allow the truth that dwells in you to control your speech and your actions. When you live and speak the truth in every situation—including the difficult ones—you will reap a multitude of blessings. For instance...

- Truth sets you free while lies enslave you to sin.

- Truth binds hearts together while deceit destroys relationships.

- Truthfulness is supernatural, while lying is an easy and natural response.

- Truthfulness points you heavenward while lying lowers you to the deceiver's level.

- Truthfulness is a grace that never goes out of style, while lying leads only to disgrace.

- A truthful woman will always be respected. And her honesty will always honor and glorify God.

~ A Prayer to Pray ~

Dear Lord of all grace and truth, thank You for speaking the truth so I can know You, believe in You, and trust You. You are the way, the truth, and the life. Because You never lie, I can trust You. Help me to be truthful and trustworthy, like You are. I want truthfulness to become my way of life. Amen.

Want to Know More About... Being Truthful?

Read these verses in your Bible and write out what they say about lying and telling the truth.

Psalm 34:13—

Proverbs 12:22—

Proverbs 24:26—

Proverbs 30:7-8—

Zechariah 8:16—

Colossians 3:9—

In your Bible, read Acts 5:1-5.

Briefly state what happened in this passage.

What role did Satan play in verse 3?

Write out the Peter's final words in verse 4.

Which of these verses were your favorites or the most challenging, and why?

12

★ ★ ★ ★

Wise

Knowing the Right Thing to Do

 "Oh no, not another decision to make! What am I going to do? I need some help making the right decision."

How we wish this had been Jessica's response last week before she made her latest bad decision. If only she had stepped back, or waited before she said *yes*—or if only she had said *no*, or turned away, or asked for advice from her parents, or her youth leader, or her wise friend Wendy. But alas, she didn't do any of these things. Jessica never really thought much about which direction to take or even about the consequences of her decisions until she got caught—which was exactly what happened this past week.

Jessica was beginning to shed herself of some questionable friends. But for whatever the reason, she still chose to hang out with Cindy during lunch. Cindy had never been a good influence on Jessica, and that day was no exception. It came close to costing Jessica a suspension! Evidently while Jessica was with Cindy, Cindy persuaded Jessica that they should hide in the bathroom and experiment with smoking. Jessica didn't experiment, but she went with Cindy, and they both got caught by a teacher.

If only Jessica had the sense and wisdom to avoid people like Cindy, who tend to drag others down to her level! Choosing the right friends was just one of Jessica's problems. And then there was also Jessica's mouth, which was constantly getting her into trouble. Jessica hadn't yet learned that God has provided all the resources she needs to help her make better choices. So out of either stubbornness or ignorance, Jessica was not turning to God for His help.

Is your philosophy on decision making something like Jessica's? Oh dear, I hope not! As one of God's young women, your life doesn't have to be complicated. Many acceptable activities have already been established for you, like going to school and obeying your parents, teachers, and others in authority such as your youth leaders and sports coaches. What makes life complicated and demanding is when you do things on your own and make decisions without turning to God and His wisdom.

This seemed to be Jessica's problem. God has provided truth, wisdom, and information. Yet Jessica simply wasn't pursuing them. And anytime we choose to resist God's help, we will end up making poor or wrong choices that can lead to negative consequences that hurt our future.

But in Jessica's case, all is not lost. There's hope! Jessica is continuing to go to the youth class on the life of Jesus. She has begun to apply a lot of what she is learning about

Jesus' character qualities. Obviously, wisdom is a quality that Jessica desperately needs. So hopefully before this evening's study is over, Jessica will be able to answer the question the youth leader asked at the beginning of class: "How can you make decisions that are right and honor Jesus?"

Pastor Jon then continued, "Turn in your Bible to the Gospels as we come to another one of Jesus' character qualities, wisdom. Here again we meet up with the One who had perfect wisdom, and therefore, the One who can provide the perfect model for us to follow, Jesus Christ."

Jesus Shows You the Way

Like all the qualities we've looked at in this book, Jesus shows you the way to wisdom. In fact, He *is* wisdom. As God, He has perfect knowledge. Therefore He acts in perfect wisdom and made all the right choices. Don't you wish you could be more like Jesus and make better choices? Well, you can be thankful once again because Jesus has, in fact, shown us how to make wise choices.

What is wisdom? It is seen in

- the choices you make,

- the actions you take, and

- the words you speak.

That's what true wisdom is. All summed up, it is the correct application of knowledge. A good goal for you is to learn how to develop the wisdom you need, the wisdom that makes you more like Jesus—not only in the way you live but also in the decisions you make.

Falling in Love with Jesus

Step 1 in being wise is found in the words Jesus spoke to a man named Nicodemus. To this man Jesus said, "You must be born again" (John 3:7). Let's take a closer look at what happened.

Nicodemus came to Jesus in secret. The more Nicodemus heard about Jesus, the more interested he became in knowing more about Him. One night this respected Jewish scholar and teacher came to meet and talk with Jesus. Why at night? Maybe Nicodemus was hoping no one would see him. He didn't want to hurt his reputation on account of being seen with Jesus. But Nicodemus approached Jesus with an open and seeking heart. He believed Jesus had answers. He was a teacher himself and came to Jesus with a teachable spirit. He wanted to learn more about the man Jesus. And he wanted to learn from Him.

So here's the scene—a teacher in Israel is coming to Jesus, the source of all wisdom, to seek wisdom. What wise counsel did Jesus give to Nicodemus? He told him, "You must be born again." In other words, Jesus told Nicodemus that if he truly wanted the wisdom of God, he had to start all over. Once he was "born again" and became a believer in Jesus, he would live and act in a manner consistent with his new spiritual nature. He would experience the transforming power of salvation.

Read through Nicodemus' talk with Jesus (John 3:1-21), and do your thing! Mark what you like and what you think is important. And jot down any questions you have in the margins of your Bible.

A question for your heart: When you are born again, wisdom becomes yours in Jesus Christ. With the new birth only God can give, you receive eternal life, the power and guidance of the Holy Spirit, and wisdom. As you follow Jesus, the Lord, you become more aware of how He wants you to act. You begin applying the wisdom you're learning to your decision-making process...which means you begin making wiser choices! Your speech too becomes more careful and gracious as you choose to speak wisely.

What Jesus told Nicodemus applies to you as well: You must be born again. Is this true of you? Have you been born again? If so, I'm sure you've fallen in love with Jesus. If not, you can start your life over today and begin walking in wisdom. God will give you His wisdom to help you know the right thing to say, the right thing to do, and the right choices to make. He will personally guide your life.

And here's more good news! You can embrace Jesus and His saving grace at any time. You can be born again by receiving Jesus Christ as your Savior. Note and mark what these verses tell you about being born again and the wonderful difference it makes in your life:

> *If you confess with your mouth, "Jesus is Lord," and believe in your heart that God raised him from the dead, you will be saved* (Romans 10:9).

> *In him we have redemption through his blood, the forgiveness of sins, in accordance with the riches of God's grace* (Ephesians 1:7).

To all who received him, to those who believed in his name, he gave the right to become children of God (John 1:12).

God so loved the world that he gave his one and only Son, that whoever believes in him shall not perish but have eternal life (John 3:16).

If anyone is in Christ, he is a new creation; the old has gone, the new has come (2 Corinthians 5:17).

[In Christ] we have the mind of Christ (1 Corinthians 2:16).

The Quest for Wisdom

As you've just seen, the Bible says whoever is in Christ has the mind of Christ. As a Christian, Jesus gives you the ability to grow in wisdom. But that growth involves some effort from you. One of my favorite passages regarding wisdom is in Proverbs, one of the "wisdom books" in the Bible. As you read the verses, hear their message. Maybe even grab your pen and circle the verbs or actions that indicate what's involved in getting wisdom.

My son, if you accept my words
    and store up my commands within you,
turning your ear to wisdom
    and applying your heart to understanding,
and if you call out for insight
    and cry aloud for understanding,

and if you look for it as for silver
and search for it as for hidden treasure,
then you will understand the fear of the LORD
and find the knowledge of God.
For the LORD gives wisdom;
from his mouth come knowledge and
understanding (Proverbs 2:1-6).

Did you notice the word "if" as you read through the verses? How many times was it used?

According to verse 5, what happens if you do what these verses say to do?

According to verse 6, who is the source of all wisdom, knowledge, and understanding?

A question for your heart: I don't know where you are in your relationship with Jesus or in your knowledge of God's Word, the Bible. But, after reading these verses filled with dynamic actions that describe a heart that is hungry and desperate for wisdom, what changes do you need to make? What can you do to actively seek wisdom?

Falling in Love with Your Bible

I'm sure you realize by now that the wisdom of Jesus comes from knowing His Word, the Bible. A psalmist in the Old Testament understood this. As you read the cry of his heart, make a note of his emotion, his commitment to God's Word or law, and what he possessed as a result.

> *Oh, how I love your law! I meditate on it all day long. Your commands make me wiser than my enemies* (Psalm 119:97-98).

The purpose of the Bible is to describe the Person and work and character of God's Son, Jesus Christ. Jesus is revealed in Scripture. And, as you and I read the Bible, we are changed more and more into the image of Jesus. As the Bible itself declares, "All Scripture is God-breathed and is useful for teaching, rebuking, correcting and training in righteousness, so that the man of God may be thoroughly equipped for every good work" (2 Timothy 3:16-17). There is transforming power in the Word of God, which helps make our behavior more Christlike.

A question for your heart: Getting to know Jesus by reading the Bible will give you the knowledge you need to make wise decisions, better choices, and speak with wisdom. The Lord has a plan for your life—a grand plan. And as you fall in love with your Bible and read it regularly, you'll grow in wisdom. You'll become prepared for the grand plan God has for you. You'll take on the qualities Jesus possessed as you become more like Him. And you'll do the works of Jesus, who "went around doing good" (Acts 10:38). It's like this: The more you grow in your knowledge of Jesus, the more you will reflect Him, and the more you'll be like Him. And it all begins with loving Jesus and loving His Word!

Looking Up

It's hard to imagine it, but Jesus, who was God in human flesh, looked to the Father through prayer for wisdom. From what we read in the Gospels and have noted several times in this book, Jesus was constantly talking with God. He never failed to check in with His Father about the decisions He had to make and the issues that were facing Him. Jesus asked for the Father's wisdom, and even as He made His way to the cross, He prayed, "May your will be done" (Matthew 26:42).

Here's something to remember: Prayer is the path to wisdom. Whatever happens in your crazy day, ask God for help. Whenever you need to make a decision (and as you know all too well, that can mean about once every minute!), look up. Check in with God. Ask for His help. Some decisions take time, but even if you have only a split second, look straight into God's heart and ask, "Father, what is the right thing to do? What is the right thing to say?" That's what James 1:5 teaches us to do:

If any of you lacks wisdom, he should ask God...and it will be given to him.

What is the need?

What is the solution?

What is the promise?

So, in the words of Jesus, pray! "Ask and it will be given to you" (Matthew 7:7).

A question for your heart: Throughout the Bible, we read that if we want wisdom, we are to ask God for it. So, in everything we do, we should pray for wisdom. And here's a checklist of other sources of godly wisdom:

___ read your Bible

___ obey what you discover in God's Word

___ seek the wisdom of wise counselors

____ follow the examples of mature people who are already walking God's path of wisdom

Look over this list again. Check the things you are already doing. For those areas in which you need improvement, write out one step you'll take this week to grow into a wiser young woman.

Wisdom is calling out to you. Are you listening? Wisdom says, "I love those who love me, and those who seek me find me" (Proverbs 8:17). The results you reap in life will be affected by whether or not you choose to seek God's wisdom and direction. Your decisions are vitally important because of the consequences that result for you and those you know—as well as for your future. That's why it's wise to seek God's wisdom, to ask for His leading. Purpose to follow Solomon's advice in Proverbs and seek wisdom in everything you do. Make sure you ask God for wisdom on a regular basis.

Walking the Road to Wisdom

By now you know that wisdom becomes yours as you spend time in God's Word and seek His direction through prayer. But there's more for you to do. As Proverbs 4:7 declares, "Wisdom is supreme; therefore get wisdom. Though it costs all you have, get understanding."

Our Jesus "grew in wisdom" (Luke 2:52). As man, He went through all the normal growth processes. He had to grow mentally, spiritually, socially, and in wisdom. And you need to do the same and go through the same growth process. As you know all too well, wisdom doesn't come overnight. (Wouldn't that be great?) But the good news is that you can accelerate your progress by making it a goal to get wisdom. How can you make this happen? Read on. You'll see a few repeats, but they are important.

STEP #1: DESIRE WISDOM

> *Happy is the [girl] who finds wisdom...who gains understanding; For [wisdom] is more profitable than silver and returns better yields than gold* (Proverbs 3:13-14).

STEP #2: PRAY FOR WISDOM

> *If you call out for insight and cry aloud for understanding, and if you look for it as silver and search for it as for hidden treasure, then you will understand the fear of the LORD and find the knowledge of God* (Proverbs 2:3-5).

STEP #3: SEEK WISDOM

> *If you look for [wisdom] as silver and search for it as for hidden treasure, then you will understand the fear of the LORD, and find the knowledge of God* (Proverbs 2:4-5).

STEP #4: TRUST GOD'S WISDOM

> *Trust in the LORD with all your heart and lean not on your own understanding; in all your ways acknowledge him, and he will make your paths straight* (Proverbs 3:5-6).

Reflecting the Heart of Jesus

Because Jesus was perfect, He always made perfect decisions. This will not always be true of you. But (more good news!) when you choose to submit to the Father's will and follow His lead, you will reflect the heart of Jesus. You'll find yourself viewing life from His point of view. You'll begin choosing better courses of action. You'll be blessed by the results of the wisdom you're applying, and so will the other people in your life. You'll make fewer mistakes and goofs, both in your behavior and in your choices. And you'll be beautiful! One of my favorite verses regarding the beauty of wisdom is Proverbs 3:22. After telling the young reader to hold tight to sound wisdom and discretion, the writer explains, "They will be life for you, an ornament to grace your neck."

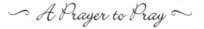

A Prayer to Pray

My wonderful Lord, You are "the wisdom of God" (1 Corinthians 1:24). You grew in wisdom, walked in wisdom, spoke wisdom, and lived in wisdom. Thank You for setting a pattern for me to follow. Help me with the choices I have to make. I pray that the way I act and the words I speak will reflect Your beautiful presence in my life...and that they will shine with Your wisdom! Amen.

Want to Know More About...
Being Wise?

Scan 1 Kings 3:3-9. After God told Solomon to ask anything of Him, what did Solomon ask for, and why?

What was the result of Solomon's request, according to 1 Kings 4:29-30?

Now scan 1 Kings 12:1-14. Meet Solomon's son, Rehoboam. Where did he turn for wisdom, according to verses 6-8?

(Just a note: After Rehoboam's failure to follow the advice and wisdom of the older, more experienced men, Israel was divided into two nations.)

What does Proverbs 9:10 say about the starting place for wisdom?

What is the plea of the father to his young son in Proverbs 5:1-2?

Write out the components of wisdom as stated in James 3:17.

Which of these verses were your favorites or the most challenging, and why?

★ ★ ★ ★

Responding with a Heart of Worship

 "What an amazing experience!" remarked Jessica as she and Wendy stood around the snack table after the final study on the life of Jesus. Their youth pastor and his wife had put together a multimedia presentation for the kids to show them highlights of their recent visit to the Holy Land. Jessica had never thought much about Jesus or about where He lived and ministered during His time on earth. So for her, this study and the video clips gave her all new things to think about.

Jessica went on, "Wasn't that cool when Pastor Jon ended with his video recording of the church service he and Rebecca went to while they were in Jerusalem?" Jessica could hardly believe that the worship service was at the very place that may have been the tomb where Jesus was buried.

Wendy felt the same way. "Oh wow, yes! And did you notice that while the group was listening to a message on the resurrection, and singing 'Christ Arose,' that the camera was aimed at a tomb carved out of a rock wall with its stone door rolled to the side? Wow, that's just like in the Bible!"

Yes, Pastor Jon had mentioned that Bible scholars didn't all agree whether this was the actual tomb where Jesus was buried. But it didn't matter to Jessica. That video presentation—done in such a worshipful way—was an amazing visual reminder to her that He has risen. What an incredible way to end their study about Jesus! *And besides that,* thought Jessica, *this Sunday is Easter! I'm getting excited just thinking about the special time of worship we'll have at church.*

Yes, Jessica was right to be excited about the Easter service coming up. With all she had learned and all the changes she had made in her life, worship could be the only response after a study on the life of Jesus. As she and Wendy walked out of the youth center, Jessica could still hear Pastor Jon's closing words. They went something like this:

> Jesus was born and lived in weakness, yet He is the recipient of all power. Jesus was the poorest of the poor, yet He owns all the riches of heaven and earth. Jesus was mocked as a fool at His death, yet He is the wisdom of God. Jesus was humiliated at His trials, yet He has received all honor and glory. Jesus was made a curse on the cross, yet He has become a blessing to all who believe. The only fitting response to the eternal plan of the Father for all the universe is to fall down and worship the Lamb of God, to worship the only One who is worthy.

Then Pastor Jon had all the kids stand and read Revelation 5:11-14 together out of their Bibles as he brought the study to an end.

> *I looked, and heard the voice of many angels, numbering thousands upon thousands, and then thousand times ten thousand. They encircled the throne and the living creatures and the elders. In a loud voice they sang: "Worthy is the Lamb, who was slain, to receive power and wealth and wisdom and strength and honor and glory and praise!"*

> *Then I heard every creature in heaven and on earth and under the earth and on the sea, and all that is in them, singing: "To him who sits on the throne and to the Lamb be praise and honor and glory and power, for ever and ever!"*

> *The four living creatures said, "Amen," and the elders fell down and worshiped.*

As Jessica left the church that night, in her mind she could still hear the group reading all those verses about Jesus. In her heart she knew she would never forget this special night—and this wonderful study about Jesus. She was sooooo thankful she had gone...and was a little ashamed of her initial attitude. Another prayer slipped out of her heart: "Thank You, dear Jesus, that You are so awesome! I love You. And I want to reflect You more and more, like a bright and shining star. Help me!"

My Prayer Calendar

Jan.	Feb.	Mar.	Apr.	May	June
1	1	1	1	1	1
2	2	2	2	2	2
3	3	3	3	3	3
4	4	4	4	4	4
5	5	5	5	5	5
6	6	6	6	6	6
7	7	7	7	7	7
8	8	8	8	8	8
9	9	9	9	9	9
10	10	10	10	10	10
11	11	11	11	11	11
12	12	12	12	12	12
13	13	13	13	13	13
14	14	14	14	14	14
15	15	15	15	15	15
16	16	16	16	16	16
17	17	17	17	17	17
18	18	18	18	18	18
19	19	19	19	19	19
20	20	20	20	20	20
21	21	21	21	21	21
22	22	22	22	22	22
23	23	23	23	23	23
24	24	24	24	24	24
25	25	25	25	25	25
26	26	26	26	26	26
27	27	27	27	27	27
28	28	28	28	28	28
29	29	29	29	29	29
30		30	30	30	30
31		31		31	

July	Aug.	Sept.	Oct.	Nov.	Dec.
1	1	1	1	1	1
2	2	2	2	2	2
3	3	3	3	3	3
4	4	4	4	4	4
5	5	5	5	5	5
6	6	6	6	6	6
7	7	7	7	7	7
8	8	8	8	8	8
9	9	9	9	9	9
10	10	10	10	10	10
11	11	11	11	11	11
12	12	12	12	12	12
13	13	13	13	13	13
14	14	14	14	14	14
15	15	15	15	15	15
16	16	16	16	16	16
17	17	17	17	17	17
18	18	18	18	18	18
19	19	19	19	19	19
20	20	20	20	20	20
21	21	21	21	21	21
22	22	22	22	22	22
23	23	23	23	23	23
24	24	24	24	24	24
25	25	25	25	25	25
26	26	26	26	26	26
27	27	27	27	27	27
28	28	28	28	28	28
29	29	29	29	29	29
30	30	30	30	30	30
31	31		31		31

Notes

1. Thomas Edison, as cited in Roy B. Zuck, *The Speaker's Quote Book* (Grand Rapids, MI: Kregel, 1997), p. 276.

2. See Luke 6:12, John 17, and Luke 22:40-46.

3. Elizabeth George, *A Young Woman After God's Own Heart* (Eugene, OR: Harvest House, 2003), p. 139, citing Roy B. Zuck, *The Speaker's Quote Book* (Grand Rapids, MI: Kregel, 1997), p. 114.

4. See Romans 5:2; Ephesians 2:8.

5. John Laidlaw (1832–1906), Scottish minister and theologian.

6. Elizabeth George, *A Young Woman After God's Own Heart* (Eugene, OR: Harvest House, 2003), p. 204.

7. Roy B. Zuck, *The Speaker's Quote Book* (Grand Rapids, MI: Kregel, 1997), p. 326.

8. Bruce B. Barton, *Life Application Bible Commentary—John* (Wheaton, IL: Tyndale House, 1993), p. 185.

9. Bruce B. Barton, *Life Application Bible Commentary—Ephesians* (Wheaton, IL: Tyndale House, 1997), p. 86.

A Young Woman After God's Own Heart

*Discover God's plan and purpose
for your life!*

What does it mean to pursue God's heart in your everyday life? It means understanding and following God's perfect plan for your friendships, your faith, your family relationships, and your future. Bible teacher Elizabeth George reveals how you can...

- grow closer to God

- enjoy meaningful relationships

- make wise choices

- become spiritually strong

- build a better future

- fulfill the desires of your heart.

Get caught up in the exciting adventure of a lifetime—become a woman after God's own heart!

Other Harvest House Books by Elizabeth George

A Young Woman's Guide to Making Right Choices

You pick your clothes, friends, and boyfriends. You decide what to do and how to act at school, at home, and at the mall. You opt to do homework and chores. You also deal with temptations such as lying, cheating, drugs, and sex.

So what's the best way to handle so many options? Elizabeth shares verses and principles from God's Word that give you sure and easy ways to make right decisions...the best decisions. You can...

- avoid trouble and bad situations
- improve your friendships
- develop confidence and character
- get along better with your family
- set standards for your friendships with guys

You'll love interacting with a today teen named Hannah, using the helpful checkpoints for choices, and thinking on insightful questions that help you understand God's wisdom and live it out.

Travel with Jesus! Love, joy, peace, patience, kindness, goodness, faithfulness, gentleness, and self-control are qualities Jesus possessed—and He wants you to have them too. Bestselling author Elizabeth George takes you step by step through the fruit of the Spirit to help you get the most out of your life. By paying attention to your journey with God, you'll be able to...

- be positive as you interact with your family and friends
- have peace regardless of the pressures of school and relationships
- experience joy even when facing difficulties
- get control over bad habits

As you walk with Jesus your life will be more exciting and fulfilling each day...in every way.

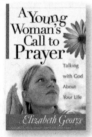

God wants to hear from you! He has given you an amazing gift—the ability to personally talk with Him every day. Through prayer, you can share with God your joys and triumphs, hurts and fears, and wants and needs, knowing that He cares about every detail of your life. Elizabeth George will help you...

- develop a stronger relationship with God
- set a regular time to talk to Him
- share sticky situations and special concerns with Him
- discover and live His will
- activate a heart that centers on Him

God is your forever friend—and He's always ready to talk with you. Experience the joy of knowing Him in a very real way through prayer.

BIBLE STUDIES *for* BUSY WOMEN

Character Studies

Old Testament Studies

New Testament Studies

A WOMAN AFTER GOD'S OWN HEART BIBLE STUDIES

*E*lizabeth takes women step-by-step through the Scriptures, sharing wisdom she's gleaned from more than 30 years as a women's Bible teacher.

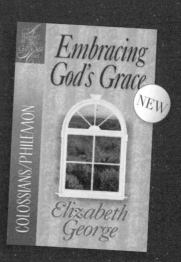

• MINUTE FOR BUSY WOMEN •

Elizabeth George can also be heard on the radio with her feature "A Woman After God's Own Heart."

Books by Elizabeth George

- Beautiful in God's Eyes
- Breaking the Worry Habit...Forever
- Finding God's Path Through Your Trials
- Following God with All Your Heart
- Life Management for Busy Women
- Loving God with All Your Mind
- A Mom After God's Own Heart
- Quiet Confidence for a Woman's Heart
- The Remarkable Women of the Bible
- Small Changes for a Better Life
- Walking with the Women of the Bible
- A Wife After God's Own Heart
- Windows into the Word of God
- A Woman After God's Own Heart®
- A Woman After God's Own Heart® Deluxe Edition
- A Woman After God's Own Heart®— A Daily Devotional
- A Woman After God's Own Heart® Collection
- A Woman After God's Own Heart® DVD and Workbook
- A Woman's Call to Prayer
- A Woman's High Calling
- A Woman's Walk with God
- A Woman Who Reflects the Heart of Jesus
- A Young Woman After God's Own Heart
- A Young Woman After God's Own Heart—A Devotional
- A Young Woman's Call to Prayer
- A Young Woman's Guide to Making Right Choices
- A Young Woman's Walk with God

Study Guides

- Beautiful in God's Eyes Growth & Study Guide
- Finding God's Path Through Your Trials Growth & Study Guide
- Following God with All Your Heart Growth & Study Guide
- Life Management for Busy Women Growth & Study Guide
- Loving God with All Your Mind Growth & Study Guide
- A Mom After God's Own Heart Growth & Study Guide
- The Remarkable Women of the Bible Growth & Study Guide
- Small Changes for a Better Life Growth & Study Guide
- A Wife After God's Own Heart Growth & Study Guide
- A Woman After God's Own Heart® Growth & Study Guide
- A Woman's Call to Prayer Growth & Study Guide
- A Woman's Walk with God Growth & Study Guide
- A Woman Who Reflects the Heart of Jesus Growth & Study Guide

Children's Books

- A Girl After God's Own Heart
- God's Wisdom for Little Girls
- A Little Girl After God's Own Heart

Books by Jim & Elizabeth George

- God Loves His Precious Children
- God's Wisdom for Little Boys
- A Little Boy After God's Own Heart

Books by Jim George

- 10 Minutes to Knowing the Men and Women of the Bible
- The Bare Bones Bible® Handbook for Teens
- The Bare Bones Bible® Handbook
- The Bare Bones Bible® Facts
- A Husband After God's Own Heart
- A Man After God's Own Heart
- The Man Who Makes a Difference
- The Remarkable Prayers of the Bible
- A Young Man After God's Own Heart

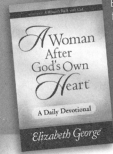

About the Author

Elizabeth George is a bestselling author who has more than 6.5 million books in print and is a popular speaker at Christian women's events. Her passion is to teach the Bible in a way that changes women's lives.

For information about Elizabeth's speaking ministry or to purchase her books visit her website:

www.ElizabethGeorge.com

or call 1-800-542-4611

Elizabeth George
PO Box 2879
Belfair, WA 98528